BEYOND THE FALLING SKY

BEYOND THE FALLING SKY
SURMOUNTING PRESSURES ON HIGHER EDUCATION

Edited by Thomas M. Stauffer

AMERICAN COUNCIL ON EDUCATION
Washington, D.C.

Library of Congress Cataloging in Publication Data
Main entry under title:

Beyond the falling sky.

   Thirty-three papers presented at the 1980 annual meeting of the American Council on Education in San Francisco.
   Includes bibliographical references.
   1. Education, Higher—United States—Congresses.
I. Stauffer, Thomas M.   II. American Council on Education.
LB2301.B49   378.73   81-12726
ISBN 0-8268-1460-X   AACR2

9 8 7 6 5 4 3 2 1

Printed in the United States of America

CONTRIBUTORS

Alexander W. Astin
Professor of Higher Education, University of California, Los Angeles;
President, Higher Education Research Institute

Blanche D. Blank
Professor of Political and Social Sciences, formerly Vice President
for Academic Affairs, Yeshiva University

Howard R. Bowen
Professor of Economics and Education, Claremont Graduate School

Richard P. Chait
Associate Provost, Pennsylvania State University

Dean Chavers
President, Bacone College

David W. Ellis
President, Lafayette College

Carolyn L. Ellner
Associate Dean, Claremont Graduate School

Joseph R. Fink
President, College Misericordia

Theodore Freedman
Director, National Program Division, Anti-Defamation League
of B'nai B'rith

Ivan E. Frick
President, Elmhurst College

Richard C. Giardina
Associate Provost for Academic Programs, San Francisco State University

I. Michael Heyman
Chancellor, University of California, Berkeley

William J. Hilton
Director, Lifelong Learning Project, Education Commission of the States

Dean C. Jackson
President, Navajo Community College

Walter Jewell
Secretary to the University, University of New Haven

Elizabeth H. Johnson
Commissioner, Oregon Educational Coordinating Commission,
and Member, Educational Issues Committee

Dennis P. Jones
Associate Director, National Center for Higher Education
Management Systems

David J. King
Dean of the College of Liberal Arts, Oregon State University

Moses S. Koch
Formerly President, Monroe Community College (N.Y.); Dean,
College of Human Development and Learning, Murray State University

Arend D. Lubbers
President, Grand Valley State Colleges

Patricia Porter McNamara
Research Analyst, Higher Education Research Institute

Robert C. Maxson
Senior Vice President for Academic Affairs, University of Houston System;
formerly Chancellor, University of Houston at Victoria

Elbert W. Ockerman
Dean of Admissions, and Registrar, University of Kentucky

Paul J. Olscamp
President, Western Washington University

John F. Reichard
Executive Vice President, National Association for Foreign Student Affairs

Leonard M. Rieser
Provost, Dartmouth College

Bernice Resnick Sandler
Executive Associate, and Director of the Project on the Status
and Education of Women, Association of American Colleges

Eldon G. Schafer
President, Lane Community College (Ore.)

Charles E. P. Simmons
President, Lake Erie College

Ralph Z. Sorenson
Formerly President, Babson College; President and Chief Executive
Officer, Barry Wright Corporation, Watertown, Maine

Thomas M. Stauffer
Director, Division of External Relations, American Council on Education

Ronald S. Stead
Executive Director, Presidential Search Consultation Service,
Association of American Colleges and Association of Governing Boards
of Universities and Colleges

Ruth G. Weintraub
Senior Vice President, Academy for Educational Development

Jacqueline Grennan Wexler
President, Academic Consulting Associates, Inc.

CONTENTS

FOREWORD

To those responsible for their solution, the problems confronting higher education often seem almost overwhelming. Despite the essential role played by America's colleges and universities in the nation's political fabric and economy, resources have always been lacking to deal adequately with major academic problems. In the present environment, pressured by inflation and harassed by public demands, the problems seem to loom larger than usual to academic leaders. They are forced to forgo the long-range view and concentrate on survival.

In our technologically based, socially dynamic society, American higher education has been at the frontier of national change. Always a microcosm of the nation's problems, colleges and universities, in fulfilling their teaching and learning responsibilities and in determining institutional policies and guidelines, are called upon to correct much that ails our society. This social pressure only amplifies the difficulties facing trustees, administrators, and professors, those having the solemn obligation to make higher education work.

Commentators, surveying the list of problems in higher education today, typically throw up their hands. The rhetoric of gloom, long commonplace in academic circles, has become more pronounced. A curious lack of confidence, even with a record number of students and higher education's core national and world role, pervades many campuses. Yet, higher education has overcome hard times before and will do so again. How well remains an open question.

The articles in this book look to solving problems and, in doing so, they strike an optimistic note amid all this travail. The authors are optimistic because their orientation is pragmatic. Pressures are recognized, to be sure, but the spirit the authors convey is to get on with the business. In my observation, such pragmatism has long undergirded our academic leadership, doom and gloom to the contrary. Therein lies a source of hope.

The collection of ideas in this book is particularly useful because the commonplace problematical themes of finance and governance are not the principal points of departure here. Without minimizing the importance of money and control, this volume emphasizes what can be done with present resources and governance structures. Tight money and shared control are not always excuses for paralysis.

To highlight the problem-solving emphasis among the academy's leadership, the American Council on Education commissioned articles for its 1980 annual meeting in San Francisco, which convened with the theme "Trustees, Administrators, and Professors— Surmounting the Pressures." Selected articles among those papers are included in this volume. Their constructive tone will, I hope, also typify attitudes for this decade: We will face serious problems; we will take a clear-eyed look at them; we will address them with integrity and vision; we will solve them. The American Council on Education in the 1980s is so oriented, and this volume is a contribution in that direction.

J. W. PELTASON, *President*
American Council on Education

ACKNOWLEDGMENTS

This volume reflects the collective wisdom of several hundred persons, although the authors remain ultimately responsible for what they wrote. The articles were commissioned as background papers for forums at the 1980 annual meeting of the American Council on Education. Topics included here were selected with the help of a hundred-member design committee and other officials in the higher education community. Authors, as well, were selected with their help.

During these forums, convened in San Francisco, college and university administrators, trustees, and professors in attendance had ample opportunity to express their ideas and offer criticisms of views developed in the background papers. Many papers were subsequently revised to reflect those additional points of view. The papers themselves were neither read at the forums nor distributed subsequently.

Many papers initially commissioned are omitted here because they range beyond the purpose of the present book. The papers were commissioned, however, with development of this volume in mind, which is intended, not as proceedings of the San Francisco forums, but to point up solutions to problems vexing higher education.

Staff members of the Publications Department of the American Council on Education merit recognition for contributions to the book's production. Marcy Massengale, department head, encouraged the publishing project and directed her staff in aiding its development. Gretchen Smith, Council assistant editor, had primary responsibility for supervising the copy editing and seeing the book through press. She worked with the authors and was helpful in many ways to the editor. Olive Mills, the Council's senior editor (retired), worked with her uncommon expertise on this volume, and Linda Gordon, graphic designer, was responsible for the layout and cover design, where her high standards are evident.

The editor is grateful to all contributors to this volume, first for their acceptance of this assignment and then for their willingness to update their papers and make revisions. Each author is responsible for his or her own ideas, while the editor is responsible for overall organization of this volume. Everyone involved in its production is pleased that so many distinguished contributors were willing to turn their considerable talents to problem solving and pragmatic optimism about higher education's future.

Council President J. W. Peltason gave support to the project, as did those participating in the San Francisco conference. All added strength to what is intended to be a volume of practical value for academic leaders generally, whether they be in the board rooms, offices, or classrooms of America's colleges and universities.

THOMAS M. STAUFFER

Solving Higher Education's Problems
Thomas M. Stauffer

Alice Rivlin, the highly respected head of the Congressional Budget Office, spoke at an annual meeting of the American Council on Education in the late 1970s on "the economic crisis in higher education." Her remarks demonstrated her usual insight, but she prefaced them with an observation: About ten years previously she had been asked to appear before the Council to speak on "the coming economic crisis." Yet, that occasion was not her first opportunity to speak on that subject; roughly ten years before, she first addressed a Council meeting, invited to speak on the "economic crisis." A pattern was discernible, she opined, and she wondered aloud why academics always think they are facing a "crisis."

Academic pundits revel in the rhetoric of the falling sky. Their propensity for paranoia, if their own rhetoric is to be believed, is habitual, and appears to be leading to a serious decline in morale among faculty members and administrators on campuses nationwide. Doomsday rhetoric is not the sole cause, but it is a contributing factor.

Low morale can be traced to causes affecting society generally or more isolated within higher education itself. The American academy is now of such scale and importance that it is fully exposed to pressures buffeting the American society as a whole: inflation, rising energy costs, litigiousness, alleged lack of national leadership, world interdependence, terrorism, environmental damage, and so on. It is understandable that academicians would be distressed by the manifold troubles. The more cynical observer can point in particular to the lag in academic salaries compared with the inflation rate and to the decline in living standards of professors and administrators. Academicians can help shape long-term societal trends through their teaching, research, and service, but, in the short run, they often feel helpless to chart their personal and professional destinies.

Control of higher education's fate is another matter, however. Inside colleges and universities, the direction of institutions is still in

1

the hands of academics. Harold L. Enarson, writing in 1974, when
he was president of The Ohio State University, made this point at a
time when the influence of state educational coordinating agencies
on colleges and universities was rapidly increasing. Institutions still
retained substantial maneuvering room, he said, and he ticked off a
long list of specifics.[1] Responsibility for action is not abrogated
merely because new state structures have been established. In
independent institutions, the problems are admittedly substantial,
but, again, an institution's fate rests mostly with the trustees, administrators, and professors, who govern what the institution is and what
it is likely to become.

How to maintain institutional quality, integrity, and purpose in
view of shifting demands of students (often linked to changing
demographic composition) and real economic dislocation is the
challenge facing higher education's leaders in this decade. Clearly,
though, this challenge cannot be met if a "crisis of spirit" is allowed
to overwhelm campus leadership. Such a crisis could lead to an
"inner exile"; that is, administrators and faculty members would
concentrate their energies more on personal and professional interests than on institutional goals, let alone national goals for higher
education.

"Management of decline," a term coined by economist Kenneth
Boulding, is the fashionable way some academic administrators and
observers rationalize the dismissal of their responsibilities. The
phrase's overtones imply minimal boldness and creativity and also
the inevitability of quantitative and, some would say, qualitative
erosion. Yet, one observer recently suggested that such management
is more analogous to a fire sale than to the reality of needs in
American higher education.

Despair is not justified, if the actions of many academic leaders
and the evidence in many data sets are carefully examined. The
academic rhetoric of crisis is obscuring much constructive, hopeful,
and hardworking leadership now operating on many campuses. For
example, George Low, president of Rensselaer Polytechnic Institute,
is using his institution as a catalyst for economic renewal of the
Upper Hudson River Valley; Neal Berte, president of Birmingham-
Southern College, has systematically restored to good health a
previously declining institution; Norman Watson, chancellor of the
Coast Community College District, has been a pioneer in using
television to provide educational services; Benjamin Alexander,

---

1. "What Is Left to Govern?" *Current Issues in Higher Education* (Washington:
American Association for Higher Education, 1974), pp. 162–69.

president of Chicago State University, has restored the faith of an
inner city institution in itself; and Martha Church, president of Hood
College, has led institutional reforms that give new definition to
higher education for women.

Many other examples of solid leadership at presidential and
other levels can be catalogued. Jacqueline Wexler, former president
of Hunter College, said, "The trick is to find ways of reallocating
resources and continually making improvements while constantly
contracting." And Saul Cohen, president of Queens College, remarked, "It's like walking up a down escalator." Wexler and Cohen
recognize the realities, but both are responding with fighting statements suggesting creativity and energy. This pattern is also evident
in many smaller institutions where institutional survival is in
question.

If such views accurately reflect the true national picture, then
the rhetoric of crisis does a disservice within the academy, contributing to low morale while eroding credibility with the public. Such
rhetoric also brushes aside the overwhelming evidence confirming
the central importance of American higher education to the American way of life. Colleges and universities are at the core of the
American political economy; American society, because of its technology, does not have the option of abandoning its postsecondary
institutions, though some prophets of doom ignore this plain truth.

A growing body of empirical evidence, too, is at odds with
despair. Howard R. Bowen, the eminent higher education economist
at the Claremont Graduate School, has long been an optimist about
the future of the American society and higher education's opportunity to serve new student groups.[2] Further, the Carnegie Council in
its summary volume reflects optimism and exposes many myths now
common among purveyors of negativism.[3] Professor John W.
Kendrick, perhaps the nation's most prominent student of productivity, emphasizes that investment in human capital through education
and research produces greater economic return than plant and
equipment investment.[4] Again, higher education's role is pivotal.
And Carol Frances, in *College Enrollment Trends*, demonstrates

2. *Adult Learning, Higher Education, and the Economics of Unused Capacity*
(New York: College Entrance Examination Board, 1980), 33 pp.

3. Carnegie Council on Policy Studies in Higher Education, *Three Thousand
Futures: The Next Twenty Years for Higher Education* (San Francisco: Jossey-Bass,
1980), 437 pp.

4. "Policies to Promote Productivity Growth," in *Agenda for Business and
Higher Education*, ed. Thomas M. Stauffer (Washington: Business–Higher Education Forum, 1980), pp. 44–135.

that projected declining enrollments in the 1980s—the underpinning of the pessimists—may not be inevitable.[5] She makes the case that enrollment trends will be influenced less by birth rates than by affirmative steps that academic administrators and faculty members can take to identify potential students. While traditional-age student cohorts will shrink, the total population will not. The outcomes can be shaped (they are not preordained) if specific steps are taken on behalf of institutions; Frances lists twelve possibilities. The Bowen, Kendrick, and Frances analyses, among others, contradict the falling sky mentality and therefore are bases for optimism.

Trustees, academic administrators, and faculty members face the difficult task of determining the place of their institutions on the continuum stretching from the rhetoric of fear to highly optimistic assessment. Evidence to support one view or the other is readily available, but each institution and often divisions within an institution are idiosyncratic. The mix of resources, personalities, and sense of direction will determine where these persons stand. Institutional mood will thereby be determined.

Where an institution or one of its divisions is likely to go will depend on practical response to its environment. And increasingly, American higher education is led by academic leaders with a keen appreciation for the pragmatic: careful planning and budgeting, careful analysis of options, and careful blending of policies and resources to carry out institutional missions and to create the campus environment desired. No college or university today can afford to be blasé about good management.

Pressures on American academic leaders discussed in this volume illustrate the mood pervading the board rooms and faculty and administrative offices of the nation's colleges and universities: realistic, pragmatic, and scared. The problems are real, but so is the interest in finding solutions. And that is the most encouraging sign. Faced with extraordinary pressures on resources of all kinds, the most thoughtful academic leaders appear to be abjuring the negative rhetoric while working toward answers. The tenor conveyed is that if there is a way out of current dilemmas, it is likely to be found.

Categorizing higher education's problems is difficult because the problems are many and diverse. Yet academic leaders must deal with three problem areas if their stewardship is to be effective. Institutions

5. *College Enrollment Trends: Testing the Conventional Wisdom Against the Facts* (Washington: American Council on Education, for Association Council for Policy Analysis and Research, 1980), 72 pp.

are, foremost, aggregations of working people. How people relate to one another is an ultimate determinant of an institution's success. Sadly, this simple proposition is frequently overlooked by overzealous college and university managers lacking appreciation for matters academic. Another problem area is campus climate, that is, the environment in which these people must work. A poor climate generates turbulence not conducive to intellectual endeavor. And finally, management must deal with myriad technical problems in meshing people with their environments. Success or the lack of success in any of these problem areas influences the resolution of others. Major problems and solutions centering on people, environment, and management are examined by the contributors to this book.

I. HUMAN PRESSURES

FACULTY MEMBERS

Appointment, Promotion, and Tenure— The State of the Art
Richard P. Chait

Administrators, faculty, trustees, and other decision makers in higher education seem to be on the prowl for imaginative new procedures and inventive policy options that will somehow cure all the problems associated with promotion and tenure and with academic administration more generally. The more difficult the times, the more desperate the search. With respect to that quest, I offer two observations. First, promotion and tenure may be symptoms, not problems; the decision makers themselves may be the problem. Second, there are no panaceas, only sound practices.

To elaborate on these propositions, I shall start with a puzzle. If tenure, as a policy or precept, presents a problem, why do not all colleges have a tenure problem? If the probationary period inexorably leads to tenure, why do some colleges tenure as few as one of every three members of a class cohort? If tenure inevitably leads to a tenured-in faculty, why do many colleges have tenure ratios of less than 60 percent? Are promotion and tenure policies so dissimilar from campus to campus as to account for the differences, or can most of the differences be explained by different approaches to administering fundamentally similar problems? In other words, the problems typically associated with promotion and tenure may be problems of policy execution more than problems of policy per se.

Personnel problems may derive from an inadequate policy or from ineffective administration of a sound policy. A board of trustees, a president, or a provost would be ill-advised to change people when the problem rests with policy. Unfortunately, to reason along these lines leads to a dangerous and probably unpopular converse: Maybe a college or university should change people rather than change policy. For obvious reasons, though, academicians apparently prefer to tinker with the rules rather than adjust the roster. Two illustrations may suffice.

A college permits the tenure ratio to reach a suddenly unacceptable level. Rather than remove the responsible decision makers—

frequently including the board of trustees—the college promulgates a new policy, which most often sets a tenure quota or less often declares a moratorium on tenure awards. Unable to maintain a well-balanced diet and a trim institutional profile, the college, already bloated, wires shut its jaws or embarks on a fast. In response to ineffective management, the college enacts a self-imposed limitation on managerial discretion. Another college seems plagued by unproductive tenured faculty members. Rather than ask why and how the strong saplings turned into deadwood, rather than ask who was responsible and why no one noticed or halted the process of decay, the college formulates a new policy—early retirement. With few opportunities for supplemental income, the deadwood remains and the vibrant faculty members with other options accept the generous pension plan.

I do not discount at all the significance of well-reasoned, clearly stated, and practical policies or the consequences of ill-advised and unworkable policies. I mean only to observe that the effectiveness of policy administration circumscribes the effectiveness of policy. By and large, colleges and universities are not without reasonable, even exemplary, policies and procedures concerning appointment, promotion, and tenure. Most seasoned administrators and trustees can readily identify the essential elements of sound personnel practices. They do not, in other words, lack knowledge or even technology. Rather, I hypothesize, they may lack pertinent institutional data to inform personnel decisions, adequate managerial skills to implement sound practices, and sufficiently steely spines to make difficult decisions. Against that backdrop, I offer a few suggestions for sound administration of sound policies and practices.

Proper Data for a Proper Decision

Without a sense of direction, one cannot chart progress. Without adequate data, one cannot make intelligent decisions. Financial officers develop and use operating and capital budgets; academic officers need human resources budgets. With currently available computer software, presidents, provosts, and deans should, at the touch of a button, be able to profile the faculty by age, sex, ethnicity, salary, tenure status, retirement date, even by research productivity. Data on actual and anticipated turnover due to death, disability, retirement, resignation, nonrenewal, and dismissal should also be readily retrievable. Many computerized models, when programmed with that data base, certain policy assumptions, and certain planning parameters, can simulate the effect of changes in those policy variables. Some simple models do not even require the use of a computer. Stanford, Princeton, Colgate, and Carleton, to name a few, rely regularly on these tools and techniques to map and plan the future. Not coincidentally, these institutions are not overcome with tenure problems.

Decision makers need not just data; they need the proper data for the decision at hand. With respect to promotion and tenure, most administrators provide trustees with the very same data sets that are generated to serve management even though they recognize that trustees should not serve as day-to-day managers. If trustees are supplied only with information about the credentials and quality of the candidates, how can they discuss any aspect of the decision other than the qualifications of the candidates? If, on the other'hand, trustees were furnished data on program needs, enrollment forecasts, placement histories, budgetary considerations, affirmative action goals and timetables, and departmental profiles, then a different discussion might ensue. With all due respect, trustees, and often senior academic officers, are not equipped to assess individual merit. The board should analyze the match between individual merit, as determined by faculty peers, and institutional needs, as determined by management and the board. How can such analyses be accomplished without appropriate data?

With appropriate data, informed tenure decisions should result. The observation applies as well to the start of the employment process—the appointment decision. Without adequate data on program quality, department leadership, growth potential, and market share, academic administrators are naturally inclined to replace the old inventory with a newer model. When the old medievalist professor retires, hire a new one. The more significant issue may be whether we need a medievalist at all or more than a computer scientist. Do we recapture vacancies and reallocate positions and resources on the bases of educational policies and plans? Some institutions do recall positions and even solicit bids from all departments on current vacancies. The bids themselves are useful data.

Considerations in Appointments

Candidates too need data. Most interviews occur on a one-way street: the college grills the candidate; the candidate does not grill the college. What could be worse than an inquisitive candidate? Every college should be able to share with candidates a tenure probability ratio or a tenure success rate. Mathematical formulas to compute that probability have been around for at least a decade. Candidates might be furnished, in advance, statements on criteria for promotion and tenure, a history of sabbatical leaves, and a projected outflow from the department. When candidates decline an invitation to join a faculty, the college should conduct follow-up interviews and surveys. Why did the candidate decide not to come? Was it money, workload, colleagues, location? How would the candidate improve the interview process? Such a survey would yield useful information and win the college some friends to boot.

Considerations in Promotion and Tenure Decisions

As candidates march toward promotion and tenure, the college should likewise collect and communicate information. There should be regular performance evaluations and conferences with supervisors. Where weaknesses are identified, circumstances should be structured to *use* the probationary period to remedy those deficiencies. Too frequently, I think, institutions fail to use the probationary period as policy intended: to weed out the clearly unqualified candidates long before the time for the tenure decision, and to vary assignments and activities to test in a trial period the potential and strengths of the better-qualified probationers. At the same time administrators inform candidates about progress to date, candidates should inform the college about the work environment to date. Dartmouth, and I suspect very few other colleges, do poll untenured faculty periodically about the quality of the work environment and how it might be improved to become more constructive and more conducive to productivity and excellence.

Data help provide a rationale for decisions. And with a defensible rationale, difficult decisions are perhaps a little easier to make and to explain. Data do not guarantee prudent decisions; they only enhance the odds.

Yet, with all the data and all the wisdom, decision makers also need a measure of courage. Unless someone or some committee or some board can bite bullets and on occasion swallow grenades, the data, the wisdom, and the policies will be insufficient.

Tenure decisions offer, I think, the best examples. To hold down tenure levels, simply tenure fewer faculty members. I recognize the stark simplicity of that observation. Yet that very statement succinctly encapsulates the approach many institutions have adopted to maintain tenure levels between 50 percent and 65 percent. Some administrators and trustees might hold that the way to reduce tenure levels and increase turnover is to eliminate tenure and substitute term contracts. Yet, data indicate that nearly all term contracts are routinely renewed and that less turnover results. If someone cannot say no, it hardly matters how many chances he gets to say no.

There are tenure policies and practices that foster discernment and selectivity as an institutional norm. I would like to enumerate a few, mindful that no policy or practice compels courage but some do make it easier and more probable.[1]

1. There should be clear criteria and standards, clearly communicated to all parties to the tenure decision process. The statement should identify areas of responsibilities, standards of performance, and sources of evidence.

2. There should be interim evaluations enroute to the tenure decision and some threshold evaluation at or near the midpoint of the probationary period. A study by the Southern Regional Education Board indicates that universities with systematic faculty evaluation programs are more likely to be selective at the time of the tenure decision.[2]

3. There should be multilevels of review that require the department or school to be answerable both to a larger constituency of peers outside the field but inside the college and to peers inside the field but outside the college. Review committees should assign appraisals of candidates for tenure to a subcommittee that carefully assesses the case and presents it to the committee as a whole. To allow the entire committee to be equally responsible for all the dockets is to free everyone from a sense of special responsibility for scrutinizing certain dossiers.

4. Evaluation of candidates should be approached as a matter of judgment and not a matter of measurement. The evaluators are making informed subjective judgments—not scientific measurements. Like a court, they should be collecting, reviewing, and weighing evidence appropriate to the tenure decision.

1. These suggestions first appeared in "Tenure and the Academic Future," in *Tenure: Three Views* (New Rochelle, N.Y.: Change Magazine Press, 1979), pp. 44–55.

2. SREB, *Faculty Evaluation for Improved Learning* (Atlanta, Ga.: Southern Regional Education Board, 1977).

5. There should be procedural checkpoints at each level of review so that the process does not move forward until it has been certified as procedurally errorless to that point.

6. Officers at the top—and here I mean senior faculty and administrators—have to be able to say no on narrow votes or, when need be, in consultation with the highest-level peer review committee, with whom reasons should be shared confidentially. The need is for, not gunslingers, but, rather, decision makers and humane decision makers at that.

7. Decision makers should review programs as well as people. Perhaps if institutions had regular external appraisals of programs and departments based on criteria such as quality, growth potential, leadership, and centrality to mission, and perhaps if they had regular assessments of faculty performance, then administrators would have some bases to make retrenchment decisions when such decisions are necessary. Institutions that have approached cutbacks in this manner have carried the day when sued.

In all these areas, the costs can be high to people and to institutions. There may be lowered morale, elevated blood pressures, and heightened tensions. There is a price to be paid, especially in the short run. Over the long run, though, the path of least resistance surely leads down the road to mediocrity. The latter, it seems to me, is the steeper price to pay. Administrators and trustees can decide whether to borrow against the future or to invest in the future. Each person concerned in the processes and each institution can decide whether to leave their successors dividends or debts.

Tenure at Dartmouth College
Leonard M. Rieser

The greatest concern on most campuses today is the implications for tenure in a stringent economic situation. A second concern is the extension of, perhaps in time, elimination of the mandatory retirement age. If the latter occurs, tenure will lose much of its meaning.

Each of us in higher education speaks from experiences at his or her own particular institution or type of institution. Mine is a small university named Dartmouth College for reasons that, while interesting in legal history, are not germane here. I wish to describe several Dartmouth routines to explain the vantage point from which I speak.

Like most institutions, Dartmouth has a statement defining the conditions of appointment to the faculty, voted into effect by our four faculties and by our trustees. It is titled "Agreement Concerning Academic Freedom, Tenure, and Responsibility of Faculty Members" of Dartmouth College. The first paragraph reads: "The Trustees and Faculty of Dartmouth College agree that the principle of academic freedom is fundamental to the life and work of the institution and of all who serve it in the responsible performance of teaching and scholarly pursuits." Further on, the following sentence appears preparatory to discussing possible action against a faculty member: "Both the Faculty and the Trustees acknowledge their obligation to uphold the standards of academic excellence and responsibility." Thus, in addition to the words "academic freedom and tenure," which appear in the 1940 statement of the American Association of University Professors, ours includes "responsibility."

Our procedures for reappointment, promotion, and tenure were written in consultation with department chairmen, but not submitted to vote by the faculty. They spell out clearly the responsibilities of faculty members, administrative officers, and trustees. A word that appears at every level is "judgment."

Our guidelines for determining the proportion of the faculty on tenure were voted into effect by the faculty and endorsed by the trustees. Thus, the trustees were intimately involved in revising our fundamental legal document a decade ago, and they were party to the guidelines for determining the number of tenure positions. They are kept informed of our procedures, but delegate the promotion and tenure responsibilities to management, as trustees from the corporate sector might say. Here "management" usually means administrative officers, although the trustees are fully aware and, by and large, respectful of the centrality of faculty participation in the management function. They are at times perplexed, even awed, by the role of faculty. The continuing education of trustees in tenure matters, especially as board membership turns over and new members join, is an administrative responsibility carried on in two ways.

First, as an example of the education process, the trustees have been given the full dossier of a tenure consideration—perhaps fifty pages including twenty-five letters, which are routinely solicited from recent graduates for every tenure case; letters from outside professionals at other institutions; and, of course, all departmental and administrative correspondence. We leave the trustees in some suspense by withholding the outcome of the case, having chosen one which, in our judgment, might have gone either way. Of course, compelling cases for tenure are as easy as they are rare; we did not choose one of these for trustee orientation.

A second procedure used to keep trustees informed occurs at each tenure action. In making tenure recommendations to the board, we now submit a one-page summary of the background describing strengths and weaknesses of the candidate. We are very candid so that the board members will know when they are voting on a compelling case and when the decision is clearly a judgmental, even borderline, decision. Thus, they acquire a realistic measure of our procedure and standards. Tenure votes in the board are usually, but not inevitably, unanimous.

I now turn to the department-administration relationship, particularly the relationship of the administration and the elected Committee Advisory to the President, to which a dean makes his recommendation. Incidentally, the current president and his predecessor have together rejected the committee's advice three times in a total of thirty-five years. Also, in only two cases in this decade have candidates complained to the Equal Employment Opportunity Commission in response to a negative decision. In neither case was the college found to be at fault.

The tenure guidelines agreed on by our faculty and trustees are that one-half to two-thirds of the faculty should be on tenure. We are now at 55 percent. This low proportion reflects some faculty expansion, primarily at the assistant professor level, between 1972 and 1977, a relatively tough dean, and a rigorous advisory committee on tenure commitments. Dartmouth has, not a strict tenure quota for each department, but rather a dynamic system that runs as follows. In any department, we tend to make tenure appointments at the rate of one per five faculty members per decade, modified upward for any department under 50 percent tenured. Two caveats may override: first, no truly outstanding candidate will be denied tenure; second, a few positions have been allocated to permit appointments that will advance our affirmative action goals, but not, of course, with specific designation.

Numerically at Dartmouth, we have really the worst of both worlds in the expectations of junior faculty, of whom there are clearly a large number. At Harvard, no one is promoted with tenure, although there are some exceptions. At Princeton and Brown, approximately 70 percent are on tenure, and both institutions tend to grant tenure to 15 percent of those who come initially as assistant professors. At Dartmouth, over a dozen years, 35 percent of those appointed to assistant professorships have received tenure on a faculty where the present tenure proportion is only slightly more than half. Thus, everyone on tenure track at Dartmouth feels he or she has a reasonable possibility for promotion, a situation that keeps expectations high. We decide perhaps two dozen tenure-level cases annually, so that tenure appointments become an overriding concern and permeate department life, especially in a large department where half are nontenured.

Two considerations exacerbate this situation: although almost everyone who has left Dartmouth holds an academic position elsewhere, opportunities are shrinking. With the change in mandatory retirement age from sixty-five to seventy, the attitude of junior faculty members toward aging senior colleagues is strained further, both because they fill positions longer and perhaps do so less adequately in later years. Still, tenure is an idea whose time not only came but is still here. A singularly important protection of tenure today is for the faculty member who is at odds with his or her department colleagues (not protection against arbitrary action from administrators or trustees which, as others have pointed out, does not require tenure). Faculty intolerance of an outspoken or "different" colleague, while infrequent, is very painful.

Second, and I believe worthy of review at a time of very high tenure ratios, is the aggregation of powers now associated with tenure as related to decisions on personnel, curriculum, and other institutional policies that have the potential to retard the development of our colleges and universities. Protection of academic freedom for faculty members may, in an ironic way, limit it for students. I doubt that those who gathered at the call of the professors from the Johns Hopkins University in 1913, preliminary to the organization of the AAUP in 1915, or those who wrote in 1940 expected that academic freedom and academic tenure should or could include liberty to, at times, stifle dissent between colleagues, limit dramatic new academic appointments from outside, or retard, indeed deny, curriculum changes within. While I am not one who favors exploring alternatives to tenure as defined in 1915 and 1940, I have misgivings that the aggregation of duties and powers now associated with the tenured status may make it difficult to change an institution's priorities.

Finally, if colleges and universities must continue to absorb the variety of external mandates of federal regulations, we in the enterprise will face real difficulty in realizing our several goals. Examples are affirmative action, retirement legislation, restriction on research and publication possibly related to national security, and the recent cases arguing for disclosure of confidential faculty records. All may strike a blow at tenure as we know it, no matter how well we manage our institutions internally.

Tenure—A View from the Board Room
Elizabeth H. Johnson

Salaries at most universities and colleges nowadays require 80–85 percent of the budget. Probabilities loom for reduced enrollments in many institutions and for increased costs, continued inflation, and restricted funds—everywhere. Most faculty members are already tenured or are on tenure track. I believe, therefore, the time is ripe for another look at tenure policies, criteria for staff and program reduction, and greater flexibility in planning if reductions must be made. A college president recently said to me that tenure does not guarantee job security; in fact, job security is not the goal. Tenure guarantees that a tenured professor shall be terminated only with due process.

Certainly, tenure in some form will continue, but tenure policies and the administration of tenure have been and will continue to be controversial, especially to persons outside academic circles. The lay public connects tenure with negatives, but mostly with a feeling that it protects weak or incompetent teachers, that it is a drag on improving the teaching function, and that it is a barrier to increased faculty productivity. But when such critics are pressed for suggestions for change, improvements, or alternatives, they come up short.

Almost everyone connected with higher education knows that tenure, with all its traditional and legal ramifications, has produced volumes of rhetoric, especially concerning the protection of academic and political freedom. Experts have given us hundreds of studies, thousands of opinions, and a handful of recommended changes. My perceptions about tenure were sharpened when, in 1973–74, I participated in a legislatively required review of tenure in the Oregon State System of Higher Education and an examination of options and alternatives. I learned more acutely how deep-seated this concept is in faculties, how difficult or impossible it is to make changes that affect almost all institutions of higher education, that tenure and programs are so interrelated that tenuring the personnel means tenuring the programs, and that the *administration* of tenure—not tenure itself—has created most of the problems. Thus I also know that the new realities in higher education require new thinking and action ahead of the problems; emotional reaction will not suffice, even in the short run.

As an example, let me use the fall 1980 convocation remarks by Paul Olum, then acting president of the University of Oregon, to his faculty. He was pleading for more money to stave off disastrous results in "quality," caused by forced budget reductions in the middle of the biennium. The drastic change was brought about when it became apparent the state would have a $204 million shortfall in anticipated revenue and a loss of federal revenue sharing, which had gone to local schools. As Dr. Olum described the prospects:

> The University's problem is severely compounded by the fact that a very large share of our budget goes to pay salaries, primarily to faculty, and that we have extremely little flexibility in responding to a sudden and massive budget reduction that comes after the fiscal year has begun.
>
> This has meant that at least for one year, we have no choice but to take advantage of all possible accidental factors in making reductions: leaving positions vacant, using overhead cost allowances, cutting out-of-state travel, omitting repairs and maintenance, reducing equipment purchases, cutting out convocation and lecture series support, canceling fall and winter commencements, reducing library book acquisitions, etc.

Olum told his faculty that "even though these cuts are traumatic, the University will—just barely—hang on by the skin of its teeth and make it through the coming year." These kinds of cuts and recapturing of reserves can, of course, help meet a temporary situation. After he expressed the hope that the state's financial condition might be better than when forecast, he continued, "It's the *next* biennium, though, and the prospects for further cuts that are the real threat." About future reductions, he added, "I can tell you right now and quite definitely, there would *be no way* for us to meet it except with a declaration of financial exigency, followed by a large-scale termination of people and programs."

If the university sees drastic retrenchment in the offing, steps should be set in motion now because documenting financial exigency in any publicly supported institution is a difficult process. Higher education has taken the position that the money is "out there" someplace, that the present shortfall is a temporary glitch, that pragmatic solutions will get us past the immediate shortfalls. What is the university proposing to do?

The immediate suggestions were: Lobby harder for more money, especially for an unusual 13 percent catch-up increase in salaries. Ask the state to come up with new revenues (read *taxes*—and that request in a state that, over the past quarter-century, has repeatedly voted down, by huge margins, a sales tax and any kind of major tax increase). Take money away from other state agencies, including basic school support funds and property tax relief, and give it to higher education. (Hardly a viable suggestion.) Fight.

A Hard Look at Publicly Supported Institutions

I need to preface my views by explaining that, for thirteen years, I was a member of the Oregon State Board of Higher Education, ten of them as chairman of the committee that dealt with faculty and personnel policies. Now I am a member of the state-level Oregon Educational Coordinating Commission, which is concerned with planning, from kindergarten through graduate school, both in public and private institutions. My points may be read as applying to the state of Oregon but are also generally applicable throughout the nation.

I want to discuss the problems of tenure, promotion, appointment, and "quality" (undefined by advocates of the institutions) from the perspective of what I see as *the new realities*—fiscal, educational, demographic. Then I wish to see how dealing with them must affect tenure and the administration of tenure policies by administrators, boards, faculties, and legislators.

1. In the first place we neither can nor will have business as usual. Three strong pressures are exerted against the possibility: fewer students, more competition from outside and inside, and fewer real dollars and continued inflation.

2. Because of rising costs, the need for other public services, and questions about the quality and productivity of the schools at all levels, citizens are questioning expenditures and goals.

3. A realistic look at demographics tells us several things. The numbers of young people available to go to college will decline. Many young people will go to other sources of training, of which there are a growing number of options: programs offered by CETA,

the military, business and industry, the unions, government itself, proprietary schools, and, especially, private entrepreneurs.

Adults will not make up for the losses. Even in the community colleges, which have experienced tremendous growth in enrollments in courses such as "Adult Self-Improvement" or "Other Reimbursables" and in hobby and recreation courses, we may have peaked. At any rate, we need to ask what is society's obligation to fund this kind of student and course. Should not, perhaps, many of these be offered on a self-support basis, with the institution or community college serving as "broker"? Although other markets of potential students might be entered—high school students, for example—we risk destroying public confidence in the integrity of education unless we know what each segment is in business to do and unless we have in place some codes of fair practice.

4. In my view and in the view of a growing number of persons of stature, the highest priority for the states must go to improving elementary and secondary education, especially in the junior and senior high schools. We have the twin problems of the underprepared student and the underprepared teacher. Although higher education has escaped much of the criticism, it must become more active in halting and reversing the deterioration of achievement, declining test scores, the inflated grades, the proliferation of electives, declining minimum graduation requirements, lowered standards, loss of a sense of values, cheating, and so on and on.

We have no policies for remediation. In the short range, colleges and universities must offer catch-up or remedial courses to students who are not able to perform at the college level. In the long range, colleges and universities should get out of the business of remediation except in unusual circumstances.

5. There are growing numbers and kinds of competitors for funds, students, and financial assistance: competition from business, industry, private entrepreneurs, CETA, and new kinds of nontraditional colleges. Competition is also seen within institutions and among and between departments, schools, and programs. A short list will touch some high points. Engineering, the biological sciences, and business are growing. How does an institution switch students' preferences and switch faculty members? They can't and they don't. If a program loses even a few enrollments, we say "quality" is diminished. Yet we can observe that student-faculty ratios are three to four times greater in some departments, and still we do not say quality is down. Business administration everywhere is overcrowded.

Should anything be done about this situation? Language enrollments are *way* down, yet emphasis on bilingual education and international studies is up. Are we or are we not going to respond? We have not faced up to reallocation of resources internally, nor have we examined tenure quotas and the effects on tenured-in departments.

6. The enrollment ups and downs will affect institutions differently: Institutional location greatly affects enrollments. Part-time students and part-time faculty are on the increase. The better-known, older institutions continue to have prestige and will have no trouble with numbers and FTE (full-time equivalent) formulas. Yet we have not been vigilant about realistic ceilings on them.

7. Inflation and increases in energy costs will stay with us and eat up the value of dollar increases. We have not looked realistically at energy saving and the necessity to deliver education in different ways, perhaps through the use of videotapes of required courses.

8. Most seriously, I believe we have a problem with the *lack of leadership in education*. Legislatures and governors keep turning to higher education for solutions to all kinds of problems, including a growing list that is affecting all of education. Higher education has furnished consultants to business, industry, government. But it has done little to analyze its own issues—including tenure—and come up with new thinking.

It is especially necessary to get away from parochialism and to educate the faculty, administration, and boards of trustees about the needs and problems of the entire state. We are all parochial—in our own departments, our schools, our state, our region. Lyman Glenny made this point to a meeting of Coordinating Commission and the Education Committee of the State Higher Education Executive Officers: "If every faculty member were required to read *Journal of Higher Education* or *Chronicle of Higher Education* or *Higher Education and National Affairs*, each would have a better grasp of current issues and the state's capacity to finance."

Getting the Act Together

If we could get away from fighting turf and governance issues, I believe coordinating boards could and should work more closely with institutional governing boards to develop, among other things, data analyses of things as they are and various kinds of planning documents, with a view to developing things as they might or ought to be. Together, the coordinating and governing boards could:

- Get the data out, including changes in tenure policies and in the administration of tenure.
- Force the discussion of crucial issues, inconsistencies, inequities, "gaps," and the like.
- Determine the appropriate state share of the cost of educating the state's students at each level.
- Think the unthinkable.
- Monitor the institutional process for:
  - Examination and evaluation of existing programs;
  - Developing criteria for staff reductions in case they become necessary;
  - Improving faculty productivity;
  - Building greater flexibility into the timetables that are involved in establishing financial exigency: giving a year's notice of possible program discontinuance or reduction; putting together restoration packages.
- We can't distinguish between the tenured and untenured.
- We must look ahead to where the trends are leading, and realize that decisions to tenure a faculty member mean tenuring a program. The decisions will have long-range cost implications.
- When program reviews are made and the results studied, it may mean that we must drop or merge a whole program.

Then we've got to face the "What ifs?" and especially "What if the money really isn't there?"

Considerations in Tenure Decisions

In looking at faculty productivity, at alternative methods of delivering educational services, and at faculty salary increases, our coordinating commission, though it does not deal directly with tenure, does need from the governing boards *their* tenure policies, *their* review of high-cost, low-enrollment programs, retirement policies, evaluation of performance, and many other things.

1. It's difficult to talk about tenure quotas if there is no uniform definition of "total faculty." Does one count teaching assistants *or* count just those on the tenure track? The difference between the two ways of counting makes a big difference in the percentage of faculty tenured in.

2. Does anyone lose tenure because of professional incompetence? Is there, in fact, any effective evaluation of teaching performance? or of amount of time spent on research? What steps are

being taken to improve college teaching? What kind of records are kept?

3. Are tenure decisions at the institution made against the backdrop of:

- Institutional and department tenure levels?
- Better mission and goal statements?
- Realistic enrollment data?
- Updated master plans?
- Financial reports?
- Affirmative action goals and timetables?
- Evaluation of teaching performance and the keeping of verifiable records under agreed-upon conditions?

States, institutions, boards, and commissions of all kinds face plenty of troubles these days. It will take hard work, good sense, and good-will cooperation to make the best out of infelicitous situations.

Faculty-Focused Development

David J. King

If the faculty members in any college or university today are not to some degree in a state of distress, I can think of only three possible reasons. The institution may be among the very few possessing the multitude of resources necessary to rise above all the problems confronting higher education. On the other hand, perhaps the administrators have been enormously clever either in hiding problems from the faculty or in shielding faculty from the problems. Or, finally, the faculty may be dead—at least in some senses of that term.

Many books, monographs, and articles have described in detail the dangers, problems, and even a few opportunities ahead in the next two decades.[1] In nearly every litany, the problems include

---

1. See, for example, Carnegie Council on Policy Studies in Higher Education, *Three Thousand Futures: The Next Twenty Years for Higher Education* (San Francisco: Jossey-Bass, 1980), and Kenneth P. Mortimer and Michael L. Tierney, *The Three "R's" of the Eighties: Reduction, Retrenchment, and Reallocations,* AAHE–ERIC/Higher Education Research Report, no. 8 (Washington: American Association for Higher Education, 1979).

dismal demographic trends, decreased faculty mobility, contracting graduate programs, decreased funding for scholarly activity, sharp decreases in real purchasing power for faculty members and administrators, changes in students' program preferences, alterations in the priority position of higher education for both public and private funding, and ever more onerous demands for accountability (some appropriate, some absurd). All these pressures, and others, are causing distress not only to administrators but also to large segments of the faculty, who selected careers in academe in part because they hoped to focus their attention on intellectual matters. New faculty are frequently insecure in their positions and worry (with justification) about retrenchment. More senior faculty members, while at least somewhat more secure, often feel trapped at an institution they had felt would be only a stopover on their way up the prestige ladder of academia. The "morale of the troops," to use military parlance, is low and falling.

One main effect of all these negative factors and the resulting anxiety and low morale is to increase the difficulty of inducing change. Almost everyone knows how change was accomplished in the good old days. The institution hired new faculty members, established new departments, or engaged in similar activities to bury, tuck away safely, or work around the deadwood or obstructionists who are inevitably present. Amazing progress was sometimes made by elevating a critical individual to the exalted position of "Dean of Parking." Most institutions can no longer afford this kind of tactic to any degree, and, as a result, the change is becoming even more difficult just when it is most needed. An increasingly common reaction of the faculty to their plight is the adoption of collective bargaining, a process which, with a few rare exceptions, merely places further obstacles in the path of adaptive change in higher education.

At Oregon State University we have created within the College of Liberal Arts a faculty-focused development program that addresses the problem of change. First, I shall describe briefly the college and the university on the presumption that faculty-focused development programs will and should differ according to the mission and type of institution.

The College of Liberal Arts

Oregon State University is the land-grant and sea-grant institution of the state of Oregon. It has a full-time equivalent enrollment of

approximately 16,000 students and academically is composed of a
College of Liberal Arts, a College of Science, and a number of
professional schools (engineering, agriculture, business, education,
home economics, forestry, oceanography, veterinary medicine,
health and physical education, and pharmacy). The College of
Liberal Arts houses the disciplines generally found in the social
sciences, the humanities, and the arts. In addition, it includes several
programs such as Technical Journalism, Broadcast Media, and Architecture and Landscape Architecture not frequently found in liberal
arts colleges. We have a full-time equivalent faculty of around 210,
with the head count varying between 250 and 275. Unique among
land-grant institutions, Oregon State's College of Liberal Arts does
not have, nor has it ever had, disciplinary graduate programs. It
exists almost exclusively to serve the undergraduate population both
within the college and in all other units of the university. The college
does offer an MAIS (Master of Arts in Interdisciplinary Studies)
graduate program, established fairly recently and not yet widely
utilized. Given the professional and technical programs that pre-
dominate at Oregon State, enrollment remains strong and limitations
on enrollments have had to be put in place for three of the last five
years, including 1980. This sketchy view of the institution may lend a
frame of reference for my description.

Faculty Participation

Basic to the approach is the assumption that faculty involvement
and faculty participation are both important elements in professional and institutional development and a positive aid to change.
Following are some of the ways in which this idea is being imple-
mented in the College of Liberal Arts.

A new governance structure has been installed in the college.
Basically it consists of a Faculty Council consisting of eight
members—a president, a president-elect, three faculty members at
large, and chairs of the standing committees. Standing committees
include the Curriculum Committee, the Budget Committee, and the
Personnel Committee. There is also a special Committee on Review
and Appeals. The Faculty Council is the legislative and policy-
making body of the faculty in the formation of college policy. The
council also coordinates the activities of the standing committees and
acts on the measures they bring to its attention. The only major
exception to this pattern of reporting to the council is on matters of
promotion and tenure, where the Personnel Committee makes its

recommendations directly to the dean. Under most other circumstances, the Faculty Council is responsible for synthesizing the work of the various committees before making recommendations to the administration. Prior to this form of governance, there were a number of elected committees, all reporting separately to the dean, with no real faculty-level coordination. Whether or not the new structure is an inherently better way of doing things, it was the framework developed by the faculty and put in place by the faculty after negotiations with the Office of the Dean. Of course, membership on all of the above committees and the council is by election.

Another activity involving the faculty is a long-range planning committee. In contrast to the regular governance committees, this committee is appointed rather than elected, although the council strongly supported its establishment. The committee is carefully balanced on a number of variables. Its assignment is to study the literature of higher education for at least six months, and more likely a full academic year. Then, with the dean, it attempts to see how the trends discerned will impinge on Oregon State and the College of Liberal Arts and how we might best adapt to these coming realities while maintaining the integrity of our programs.

Curricular Activities

Curricular change is another area of intense faculty effort.[2] Oregon State was fortunate in being awarded a large curriculum development grant by the National Endowment for the Humanities. This program has developed a wide variety of junior- and senior-level courses focused primarily on topics of interest to students in the professional and technical schools but employing a humanistic orientation. Four general areas have been emphasized: Northwest studies; marine and maritime studies; community studies; and science, technology, and values. Again, a principal thrust of this program is to assist the humanities faculty in the College of Liberal Arts to reach the students and faculty in the professional and technical schools by applying methods of humanistic analysis and synthesis to subjects of special interest to them.

General education is another curricular area in which we have invested time and effort. Since late 1978 the university has been a member of the General Education Models (GEM) Project, a nation-

2. Clifton E. Conrad and Jean C. Wyer, *Liberal Education in Transition,* AAHE–ERIC/Higher Education Research Report, no. 3 (Washington: American Association for Higher Education, 1980).

wide consortium of twelve institutions working under the direction of Jerry Gaff. The GEM network is developing a variety of models of general education appropriate to particular institutions. The seven-member team on our campus met once or twice a week for two years to try to fashion an effective general education program beyond the then-current system of distribution requirements. In fall 1980 they inaugurated the first phase of that program, an innovative, one credit hour, introduction and orientation to the liberal arts as a way of understanding the world we live in, a course required of all freshmen in the college. In addition, during 1980–81, the GEM Committee will focus on designing an integrative senior seminar and on ways to incorporate some of the courses developed under the NEH grant into the general education program. The members of the GEM Committee have become well read in, and greatly sensitized to, the complexities of current debates on curriculum, especially in general or liberal education. Their sponsoring of a full-year, once-per-week, lunch-hour seminar on general education open to all students and faculty members in the university has helped spread interest in improving general education at Oregon State. In addition it enhanced the committee's understanding of some complaints and concerns of professional schools to which the college had not been adequately sensitive.

Professional Activities

Still another way of promoting faculty interest in higher education problems beyond their disciplines has been the establishment of an internship program in the office of the dean. In this program, selected faculty members spend at least one term serving as interns in the dean's office. Interns select a particular area of interest (governance, promotion and tenure, budget, and so on) and develop some expertise in that area as well as being exposed to the general reviews of trends in higher education. They also are expected to participate in many of the conferences and meetings in which the dean or his staff members are involved. The response to this program has been strong, and the openings were quickly filled for the next two years.

Professional development, in the sense of attempts to improve faculty capabilities for instruction and scholarship, is an area that has grown enormously in the last ten years and is now being pursued on almost every campus. Through a generous grant from the Fund for the Improvement of Postsecondary Education, in 1980 we were entering the third year of a faculty-centered professional development program. This program takes a group of faculty volunteers, trains them rather extensively (for two quarters) in areas of professional development, and then makes their services available to their colleagues on a totally confidential basis. We have five members who have completed two years of this program, and four new members started the cycle again in September 1980. To check on the progress and to allow a reasonable evaluation of the program's effectiveness, each team .member fills out an anonymous case history for each client that he or she has served. As of June 1980, when the first five team members had been in the field for a total of five terms (quarters), we had acquired forty-seven case histories. Space does not permit elaborating on this program, but I evaluate it as highly successful. In training faculty members in the professional development program, an integral part has been focused on issues in higher education (and attendance at the annual meetings of the American Association for Higher Education), as well as the more traditional topics in professional development. At the end of the training period, two outside evaluators asked our first team members what they had personally received from participation in this program. On reflecting about the experience, they came to the realization that they themselves had been developed in the process of learning professional development.

If a count were made of the faculty members who have participated or are participating in the activities described above (and still others could be mentioned), the total would approach a goodly percentage of the entire faculty. More are being brought in all the time. Of course, not every faculty member successfully handles the challenges. Such an expectation would be unrealistic. On the whole, however, it appears that the faculty members are becoming more knowledgeable about activities in higher education and their position within the college and the university than was the case in prior years.

All of these activities or more could easily be seen as a "keep them busy" tactic of the dean while he gets on with running the college. I suppose something like that might be tried, but I doubt in the long run it would be successful. We are convinced in the College of Liberal Arts at Oregon State that raising the knowledge level of the faculty about problems and issues and options in higher education is, for us, a valid way to encourage the adaptations that will be necessary for the next two decades.

STUDENTS

The Art of Noble Influence Selling
Ivan E. Frick

What involvement should administrators and trustees have in the process of recruiting and retaining students? What policies, procedures, and strategies for recruitment and retention should colleges and universities adopt for the 1980s? In proposing some answers, I shall ignore here the important role that faculty and students carry in these matters. Administrators and trustees, in my view, have special responsibilities that they must assume, or else chance that recruitment and retention efforts will suffer. If they delay until crisis demands their attention, then the greater their difficulty in assuming their responsibilities.

Perhaps the attitude that crisis won't come to "our" campus is prompted in part by an appreciation for the diverse characteristics of the nation's three thousand institutions. Similarly, the diversity suggests caution against extrapolating guidelines from one college's experiences for many or all colleges. Programs and styles of recruitment and retention are more an art than a science, and such arts seem to thrive best in an atmosphere of optimism. This art has sometimes bordered on hucksterism and sometimes seems to rely on magic.

A more appropriate metaphor, in my opinion, comes from the arena of political influence, which suggests that colleges sell themselves and their influence to parents and to students, but with great caution and awareness of the hazards. "The Art of Noble Influence" in recruitment and retention is not intended to suggest that every person, idea, or activity can be placed into a neat scheme or system. More appropriate to the art and task are such terms as persuasion, pressure, slippage of efforts, and activities of persons with differing agenda. Recruitment and retention activities might be compared to an education association of diverse colleges that tries to arrive at a consensus of mission and organization in order to persuade a legislator to vote for legislation helpful to education. Metaphorically speaking, admissions efforts are also analogous to the activities of that education association in assisting the legislator in his campaign fund-raising activities and the legislator nobly selling his influence to develop the best educational system possible. But analogies and metaphors are not precise advice or recommendations for policies and procedures. The hints offered here include both general, commonplace suggestions and highly individual comments.

Constructive Roles

A basic suggestion is that administrators and trustees make a major investment of time and energy in developing, monitoring, and supporting policies, procedures, and strategies for recruiting and retaining students. Although this suggestion may seem prosaic, a review of board minutes and desk logs of chief administrators (other than the director of admissions) might well disclose that precious little attention is directed to such policies, procedures, and strategies. Administrators should regard the recruitment and retention of students as a concern equal in importance to concerns for maintaining financial solvency, handling conflict resolution, and adopting sound mission statements. If they accept this concern as a primary task, it will require significant amounts of time and energy. They are likely to find it easier to invest effort in achieving other objectives, for example, raising money.

Because recruitment and retention have long been an institutional activity, many administrators and trustees may assume that the effort is continuing satisfactorily. They may also think that their involvement might cause a hassle with the faculty, which all are trying to avoid. Therefore, better to leave well enough alone. Despite the risks, administrators and trustees should regard recruitment and retention as a major activity calling not only for their attention but also for periodic examination of the financial support devoted to these efforts.

A principal focus for administrators and trustees should be on helping to fashion and evaluate the policies, procedures, and strategies that govern recruitment and retention activities. These people will not do the work of the recruitment staff or of those who are involved in encouraging students to remain at their college. Rather, a key element for them will be monitoring these efforts on a regular basis and proposing appropriate revision of policies and procedures in order to conjoin student needs and institutional objectives as constructively as possible.

Potential Conflicts with the Faculty

At this point a principal area of conflict emerges: in matters of recruiting and retaining students, faculty objectives and institutional needs may not completely match or they may be on a collision course. During my ten years as a faculty member in the 1950s, conversations with colleagues in the coffeeshop often implied that students were never quite worthy of our most noble efforts. The feeling still persists that entering students lack sufficient motivation, ability, and academic achievement to make "satisfactory" progress. For example, the faculty often claims that the only honorable solution is to raise sharply the median established for college board scores of the entering class, and to refuse admission to many applicants who would at present be accepted. Thus conflict arises. On the one hand, the euphemistic assertion is that colleges are enrollment- or tuition-driven enterprises; on the other hand, a lack of students will create a budgetary squeeze so that another faculty goal—remaining employed—may not be achieved.

At the worst on this collision course of mismatch of faculty and students, faculty will not tailor their teaching to students' interests and needs, nor will they teach suitably for the students' entry-level abilities and skills. From the faculty point of view, accepting the entry-level abilities and skills of the students would require serious dilution of educational goals and objectives. In such conflicts, administrators and trustees have a special responsibility to see that the campus dialogue speaks to maintaining academic standards while promoting learning that begins with student interests, abilities, and skills.

These concerns are complex, sometimes contradictory. In some cases, conflicting objectives are developed. The cluster of issues posits strong academic standards and the integrity of the institution against the outcomes of learning, impact of the institution on students (especially faculty impact), and students' interests and motivation. All constituent groups in a college should work to maintain and enhance strong academic standards. At the same time, all groups should foster learning for a generation of new students, students with interests, feelings, and concerns that many of us will not have because of the generation gap.

Responsibilities for Policy and Oversight

The complexity of the issue may be further illustrated by examining the role administrators and trustees should play in determining whether their college should recruit and retain adult learn-ers, commuting students, and nontraditional students, or instead should be a residential liberal arts college for traditional college-age students. Although not every institution should recruit a diverse student body, the policy decision must be made. If the policy is diversity (whether more or less), some faculty members are likely to wish that the enrollment were really composed of 18–23-year-old residential students. Once the policy decision is made, such matters as kinds of programs and program offerings must be addressed. Again, trustees and administrators should be deeply involved in decisions that affect the mission of the college.

If a college decides to recruit the nontraditional student, it faces other questions. Shall off-campus programs be offered? If the answer is yes, then the college enters even more difficult determinations about policy and institutional management. For example, both regional accrediting associations and state boards of control are showing increasing concern about off-campus programs. An *Educational Record* article suggests that in this matter higher education faces a watershed or a watergate, and the Carnegie Council's *Three Thousand Futures: The Next Twenty Years for Higher Education* describes the issues in detail.[1]

In monitoring the procedures and strategies, administrators and trustees should periodically evaluate certain key elements: quality and quality standards of the academic programs; the admissions team's effectiveness in preparing and circulating a recruitment plan that states with clarity specific goals for recruiting appropriate students; and the team's continued effectiveness in communicating information on recruitment activities, especially to the faculty and administrative staff.

The plan and programs for retaining students need similar monitoring. The program may begin with monitoring dropouts and transfers and then turn to examining the effectiveness of the finan-cial aid program in retaining students. At many colleges the first reason students give for dropping out is lack of money. Expert financial aid counseling is critical. Further, the chief financial aid officer must exercise grantsmanship in obtaining federal student aid funds and equally exercise care in administering the funds.

In the institutional program for retention, concern for many

1. Warren M. Zeek, "Higher Education: Watershed or Watergate," *Educational Record*, Summer 1980, pp. 40–45; and Carnegie Council on Policy Studies in Higher Education, *Three Thousand Futures* (San Francisco: Jossey-Bass, 1980), pp. 98–102.

other activities must be continually exercised. How effective are the learning centers available to all students? In what ways are student attitudes and expectations handled and nurtured? Is the quality of the learning environment maintained to promote academic advising that is creative? Even all these examinations and efforts may not fully disclose why students leave an institution.

Some Pointers

In the category of idiosyncratic hints are the following. No administrator or trustee should look for easy solutions or quick fixes in solving recruitment and retention problems. Trustees and administrators may be tempted to suppose that quick fixes should be used: fire the director of admissions when recruitment is not going well; hire a public relations firm to give the institution a new image; or, even, appropriate sizable amounts of unfunded institutional aid to sell the institution's influence. These solutions may be considered but not quickly, and only rarely are they adopted.

Every effort should be made to separate the recruitment efforts from the activity of forecasting enrollment, even though the chief admissions officer must agree that the number of new students forecast is an attainable number. If the admissions officer becomes the institutional research officer who forecasts enrollments, the college community may regard the forecasts as the recruitment goals of the admissions office, and any decline from the forecast as lack of aggressive action by the admissions office.

Administrators and trustees should be wise enough to appropriate from all sources good ideas for presenting the college to prospective students and interpreting the plans to on-campus groups. It is especially important to maintain communication with the faculty but to do so without becoming embroiled in unfortunate semantic battles. For instance, ideas may be gained from Kotler's *Marketing for the Non-Profit Organization* and Montana's *Marketing in Nonprofit Organizations*.[2] My own view is that terms such as "prospective students" instead of "consumers" and "an organized plan for student recruitment and retention" rather than "a marketing plan" are still usable. The plan may be packed with insights from such persons as Kotler and the contributors to Montana's book, but academic phrases may help avoid getting into semantic battles that

2. Philip Kotler (Englewood Cliffs, N.J.: Prentice-Hall, 1975); and Patrick J. Montana, ed. (New York: Amacom, 1978), pp. 159, 172.

marketing terms cause to rage on campus. My attitude toward these semantic battles is "A plague on all your houses!"

Recruitment and retention cannot be left to fate or chance if the goals are to be achieved. The program has to be planned thoroughly, monitored carefully, and revised as needed.

A final hint: Administrators must be sensitive to, but not para- lyzed by, campus tensions that emerge in developing any recruit- ment plan. Faculty interest and efforts are sorely needed in recruitment and retention activities, starting even as early as the most basic policies are being developed. Faculty efforts are needed later, too. Conflicts may emerge in basic policy discussions and bring paralysis to the academic community. The discussions will probably bring conflict, but they need not bring paralysis.

A college can strive to practice the art of recruiting and retaining students with imagination and skill, and succeed in producing new and creative results. The future of many independent institutions may well depend on how well those institutions develop the art.

Ethical Practices in Recruitment and Retention
Elbert W. Ockerman

Given the facts already available about the decline of the traditional freshman applicant pool in the 1980s and 1990s, two of the most significant challenges to higher education will lie in student recruitment and student retention. I do not share the doom-and-gloom predictions of many authorities today. Nor do I buy the efforts to explain away the dire estimates of the immediate and long-range future. Probably somewhere in between is a balance that all of us in higher education are challenged to achieve.

Within the context of conditions as they are and are likely to be for several years, I submit that a primary concern in student recruitment and student retention is a matter of ethics.

Student Recruitment
By far my greatest concern about recruitment is what has already happened and what is likely to happen at an accelerated rate—the lack of focus on ethics in recruitment. I see top administra-

tive officials, including admissions officers, engaged in a numbers game. This game will eventually be lost. Let me cite an institution with which I am familiar. There, playing the numbers game began about three years ago. Until then, admssions were handled as a reasonable, orderly process of deadlines and a genuine commitment to good service to applicants. Just three years later there were no meaningful deadlines. The quality of the entering student group dropped. The dropout rate had accelerated. And the numbers of entering freshmen were only minimally larger than when the deterioration set in. These indicators in combination, to me, connote unethical conduct.

Pressures from the top and below are being exerted to modify admission standards and in the process change the institution's image. Philosophical considerations, if they ever existed, have either given way to questionable change or have been almost entirely abandoned. Without an adequate statement of philosophy consonant with the institution's purposes and mission, no meaningful admissions program will long survive. Here, again, is a lack of proper ethical practices.

I am increasingly concerned about the base of authority for admissions officers as they attempt to carry out effective student recruitment programs. On some campuses, adjunct and sometimes entirely separate units have emerged and thus eroded the base of authority for the admissions office. Although institutional organizational changes are, of course, necessary and frequently appropiate, the sensitivity of the admissions function limits latitude for major organizational changes. The structure of the admissions office in relation to its recruitment function requires that either it "be in charge" and held accountable or not be in charge and not held accountable. Minority recruitment efforts are important. Retention efforts are highly important. Institutional planning within the college or university, including the admissions area, is a must. However, the answer to our student recruitment concerns cannot be found in establishing separate function units that have no responsibility to or coordinating relationship with the admissions office. Indeed, organizational patterns do need to provide a base of authority and, always, an ethical focus.

Another critical factor in the recruitment-admissions process, to me, has really strong ethical implications. I know full well that the simplified admissions process for freshman applicants that we pioneered at the University of Kentucky several years ago strikes terror in the hearts of some of my colleagues. The process places full dependence on a single document that we receive from the applicant through one of the major testing agencies. No high school transcript and no application for admission are required as long as certain conditions obtain. After several years' experience with the simplified system, we know that it works. Thousands of pieces of paper are eliminated (we have not bought a filing cabinet in ten years). The applicant pool has been significantly increased. Service to the applicant is expeditious and definitive. I cannot understand why open-admission community colleges in particular have in the main not adopted a simplified admissions system. The game for the future is access to our institutions. Students will reject the institutions (and they should) if the process is complicated, involves long delays, and thus seems to hold the applicant always at some distance from the heart of the institution.

A companion to simplification of the application-for-admissions process is coordination. The admissions process is sequential. It must move from the preadmission (recruitment) stage, to the application for admission, to relationship to an academic unit, to an orientation program (if one is held), and finally to registration. Often intertwined with this sequential process are, at a minimum, student housing, financial aid requests, and a health service relationship. The admissions process and the service functions are inextricably linked. They must be coordinated. Potential students look upon an institution as a single entity, but through separate applications, different deadlines, and often no integrated data bases, the institution becomes perceived, I am sure, as a collection of different units where the right hand doesn't know what the left hand is doing. How devastating this impression is to student recruitment. How unethical it is to those who want access to our institution. Presidents must see that coordination occurs. This is the least that can and should be done.

The time has now come, indeed it is in my judgment long past, when interinstitutional cooperation in student recruitment must be brought to some order and design. Examples abound of how "the system" works when a high degree of competitiveness is injected into recruitment. The gamut runs from attempts to outdo one another in publications, to the use of financial aid as bait, to several institutions traveling over the same market time and time again, to invading other "territories" for outreach programs and duplication of program offerings, and to real hard-sell techniques. Positive, planned marketing is a must for the 1980s. It should be done on a cooperative and ethical basis, with institutions joining hands to accomplish common goals.

One final point that can have significant ethical overtones is the role of for-profit commercial agencies. Almost five years ago in my role as vice president for admissions and financial aid of the American Association of Collegiate Registrars and Admissions Officers, I urged one of our professional committees to look at the problem of the emergence of commercial agencies, which I felt would be significant in the 1980s. The committee failed to reach a consensus, and the project was for all intents and purposes dropped. There are good for-profit commercial agencies that can assist the student recruitment process. There are others, probably larger in number and certain to increase, that are not what we need at all in student recruitment. Great caution must be exercised in acquiring the services of commercial agencies. Ethics can be a significant factor and thus hold potential trouble for us.

Student Retention

After many years of languishing in the hidden areas of the vocabulary in higher education, *retention* now seems to be a most acceptable term. We have known for a long, long time that the best and most ethical recruitment tool is an effective program of student retention. Yet many of us have totally ignored this fact, and most of us have been unwilling or unable to define student retention. I can count on the fingers of one hand the institutions that have done anything significant enough to come to public attention.

Student retention efforts, in my opinion, must begin with a careful, analytical, ethical study on a longitudinal basis of what has obtained in retention at the institution and perhaps at other institutions. The process can be painful but is critically important to planning an effective student retention program. It goes directly to the heart of adequate programs, effective advising, good teaching, the presence of a strong service orientation, and an ethical student recruitment program or the lack thereof. Retention efforts must be institutionwide. A college or university cannot respond to the need for improved retention simply by setting up an office with focus on this area. If an institution has an open admissions policy, it must guarantee to students who are marginally qualified that it also has adequate developmental resources to meet their needs. At the other end of the spectrum, each college or university has every right and the need to know why it may be losing superior students.

An admissions and registrar's office can do a number of things beyond the recruitment stage to facilitate retention, and it must be involved. My office, for example, without waiting for directions and requests from other administrative units, has completed several detailed retention studies. We also have taken other steps to identify where our office can make its contributions to a campuswide effort. On the market now are student opinion questionnaires that are most helpful in initiating or accelerating retention programs. I am most familiar with those produced by the American College Testing Program. We have used two of the instruments and plan soon to introduce at least two others. We need to know much more than appears in statistical tables. One good approach has been to go directly to withdrawn students, to alumni, and even to students who plan to enroll so as to ascertain their perceptions and expectations of our institution.

In a sense I come back to the point with which I began. It is a plea that colleges and universities, and particularly the admissions officers, not become so absorbed by the desire for numbers that we allow most of our student recruitment and retention efforts to be dominated by the numbers.

The "Joint Statement on Principles of Good Practice in College Admissions and Recruitment," which includes also retention in general, is an ethical guide that every institution can and should abide by.[1] We can and must operate ethically even under the significant pressures we all face together. We do so by diminishing the emphasis on numbers; by establishing a consistent institutional and admissions philosophy; by simplification and coordination of the admissions process; by programs of interinstitutional cooperation; by having effective organizational patterns; and by a strong commitment to student retention.

1. The statement was endorsed on June 29, 1979, by the Board of Directors of the American Council on Education. It was approved by the American Association of Collegiate Registrars and Admissions Officers, the College Entrance Examination Board, the National Association of College Admissions Counselors, and the National Association of Secondary School Principals.

Copies of the statement are available on request to Office on Self-Regulation Initiatives, American Council on Education.

Conditions for Expanding Adult Learning
William J. Hilton

The range of state activity in support of postsecondary education is so broad that I must describe where my organization and I fit into the picture. The Education Commission of the States (ECS) is a nonprofit, Denver-based, interstate compact working to improve American education at all levels. Toward that goal, ECS conducts research, serves as an information clearinghouse in support of state education and political leaders, and administers projects to help the states gain vital experience in managing a variety of special education issues and problems.

My current project is a three-year, Kellogg-funded effort called the ECS Lifelong Learning Project. My staff and I work with six pilot states and as many as twenty-seven associate states to develop collaborative planning to further adult learning. State higher education executive officers serve as catalysts for bringing together a variety of representatives from public and private agencies, institutions, and organizations to assess the need for public policies and programs that will advance the cause of adult learning. Our hope is that these state-initiated planning activities will help the nation, over time, to move appreciably closer to the goal of becoming a truly "learning society."

In financing higher education in general, state education leaders, I believe, have been increasingly concerned about two matters. The first is maintaining a viable level of state support for higher education despite declining public revenues, inflation, spending ceilings, and competition from other legitimate claimants to public support. Second, they are deeply interested in working with local education officials to determine how education dollars received from state legislatures and the federal government should be spent to achieve maximum benefits. As states enter the "era of declines," their best options for spending the resources are likely to include the following: support for student assistance programs; freedom and diversity of institutional choice (forty-three states now provide substantial support to private colleges and universities); new educational technologies that promise to reduce the cost of extending educational opportunities on a broader scale; and promotion of increased effectiveness and efficiency in using facilities and resources.

With reference to the new adult learning clientele, a growing number of states are exploring avenues of public support for the adult learning movement. Matters being explored include more equitable treatment of part-time students (who tend to be adults) through student aid programs; the administrative cost of running nontraditional programs; financing noncredit, off-campus activities on the same basis as credit, on-campus offerings; and promoting new teaching methodologies, research, and program designs.[1] Although I cannot present a current assessment of state practices in each of these areas, our project's Technical Task Force has established a special subcommittee that will be looking at state policies and practices in all these areas and will periodically report its findings.

Meantime, let me present some thoughts on future funding initiatives by the states for lifelong learning. They might well be presented as four *conditions* under which state support for adult learners is most likely to be increased.

First, the climate between local postsecondary institutions and the state coordinating and governing boards, with which many of them necessarily relate, must be improved. The ECS project affords a rare and valuable opportunity to do something that will strengthen the "uneasy partnership" between state agencies and institutions. Furthermore, the opportunity comes just when public pressures for accountability are likely to force many state agencies to tighten their planning, review, and approval procedures—much to the dismay of many campuses. In such times as these, institutional leaders need to be reminded that the states are genuinely interested in working *with* colleges and universities to expand opportunities for adult learning. As confirmation, thirty-three states have expressed interest in being identified with the project, which stresses establishing a dialogue with institutions and agencies in this area of planning. My sense is that, in joining the project's effort, the state leaders are eagerly seeking a forum in which they can work with institutional leaders.

I urge several direct suggestions on institutional leaders: Seek out the Technical Task Force members in your home state. (Names and addresses are available from the project.) Participate in the efforts that many of these officials are undertaking to collect and analyze data about adult learning trends in your local communities. Remember that while, on the national scale, adult students may not compen-

---

1. See Richard E. Peterson and associates, *Lifelong Learning in America: An Overview of Current Practices, Available Resources, and Future Projects* (San Francisco: Jossey-Bass, 1979).

sate for declines in traditional enrollments, in certain states and substate areas, this market may determine the survival of an institution. If for no other reason than self-defense, you should make it your business to know what your state is attempting to accomplish in this area.

Second, campuses, like government agencies, must look seriously at the possibility of expanding *private investment* in the area of lifelong learning. Interest in promoting education-business cooperation is increasing, although some educators resist this movement lest it cast too great a vocational tint on the higher education enterprise.

Third, institutions must do more to build grass-roots support for extending adult learning services. Legislatures are suspicious of institutional appeals on behalf of adults because they know about the enrollment problems. Institutional leaders may not be the right people to sell legislators on the idea of increased public support to lifelong learning, but state agencies also might be perceived as being biased toward colleges and universities. In these uncertain economic times, public policy from the top down may be passé. We in higher education need at least to explore the value of policy development from the bottom up, by working to ensure that the public understands what we mean by lifelong learning. The public needs to realize that most of them already are or ought to be lifelong learners. Its members need to gain an appreciation of the lifelong learning concept, and come to understand the extent and importance of the unmet needs in this area and how those needs might be most efficiently addressed through public action.

Fourth, institutional offerings must be more *client-centered.* Campuses must recognize that they are not in business solely to provide jobs for the faculty or simply to preserve the status quo of academe. Stated another way, they must reassess the value of traditional education in this age of rapid technological advancement. Where traditional educational values are clearly worthy of preservation, an effort must be made to prove their worth to the new, nontraditional student clienteles, who lack perspective on the real value of college education. A client-centered approach encompasses many considerations: faculty development, including greater awareness of adult developmental needs; administrative reform (Down with Mickey Mouse registration procedures!); and reforms in student financial aid practices on the campus, so that older learners are not handicapped on that basis alone in the competition for award dollars.

I wish I could say that clear state policies focused on adult learning were evident, but I can't. Equity is a federal concern, and most states, so far, seem content to leave it at that level. My guess is that interest in consistent state policies will grow as the public investment in adult learning grows. That stage is unlikely to come about until we in higher education have contributed our share to create at least the four conditions I have described.

Nontraditional Students in Small Liberal Arts Colleges
Joseph R. Fink

In its final report, the Carnegie Council on Policy Studies claims that the next two decades will be a "golden age" for America's college and university students. According to the report, "Students will be recruited more actively, admitted more readily, retained more assiduously, counseled more attentively, graded more considerately, financed more adequately, taught more conscientiously, placed in jobs more consistently. . . . They will seldom, if ever, have it so good on the campus."[1]

This happy situation for students is projected from the demographic characteristics of the 1980s. The characteristics include a significant decline in enrollments at colleges and universities because the 18–24-year-old population will dwindle substantially during the 1980s. Although the decline in numbers will vary among regions and will have a mixture of effects on different types of institutions, the decline in enrollments will be felt by all segments of higher education.

These unpleasant realities have already led numerous colleges to modify their missions. In response to the decline in numbers of traditional students and the resulting stress on operating budgets, they have decided to bolster their enrollments by seeking nontraditional students. During the late 1960s and early 1970s, a significant

1. Carnegie Council on Policy Studies in Higher Education, *Three Thousand Futures: The Next Twenty Years for Higher Education* (San Francisco: Jossey-Bass, 1980), p. 53.

number of them, recognizing what lay ahead, began to develop continuing education programs for nontraditional students. K. Patricia Cross, who has studied the phenomenon, believes that "since the beginning of this decade, the increase in both credit and non-credit programs for adults has been nothing short of spectacular." According to Cross, "the majority of colleges in the United States now offer encouragement to part-time degree candidates and the number of colleges offering non-credit programs has more than doubled in recent years."[2]

What are the problems posed to small liberal arts colleges by mixing the older, more mature adult student population with traditional college-age students? The nontraditional students fall essentially into two categories: recent high school graduates who normally would not attend college because their preparation and ability to do the work is questionable; and more mature adults, many of whom have already had some credit or noncredit college-related experience. In many instances, the problems the colleges face are similar to those encountered when significantly large numbers of inadequately prepared post-high-school students were admitted. In many other instances, the problems are quite different.

Administrative and Organization Adaptations

In the last decade or more of developing continuing education programs, the small liberal arts colleges have established or expanded evening class offerings. They have also turned to newer forms such as weekend colleges, elderhostels and other programs for senior citizens, and specialized training programs for professional organizations or industrial employees. Unfortunately, these programs have had limited success. In many cases, the colleges have enrolled nontraditional students primarily as a counterbalance to the decline in traditional enrollments rather than as a positive commitment to a modified mission. The commitment to the nontraditional students has been less than wholehearted, and the institutions have made only minimal changes in their organization and operations to accommodate their new clientele.

Failure to change has created a series of attitudinal and organizational barriers that hamper the mature students from successfully

2. Cross, "The Adult Learner," in *The Adult Learner*, Current Issues in Higher Education, 1978, no. 1 (Washington: American Association for Higher Education, 1978), p. 2.

participating in the educational enterprise at small liberal arts colleges. They confront barriers from the time they matriculate until they graduate. To cite a few: the admissions process, financial aid, academic advising, administrative services, curriculum, scheduling, student services. More important, however, are the barriers of attitude erected by faculty members and administrators, who are more comfortable dealing with 18–24-year-olds.

When a small liberal arts college decides to admit significant numbers of nontraditional students, it must also be prepared to modify significantly its institutional management.

Admissions. Traditional admission procedures must be changed. SAT scores, high school records, and in many cases college transcripts are virtually meaningless as indicators of how well an adult student will do. Motivation is far more important, and colleges need to devise means to admit and evaluate adult students without relying on ten-year-old credentials. Policies must be adopted regarding not only the transfer of credit from other colleges and universities but also the evaluation of credit for programs conducted by business and industry. The colleges need a system for evaluating individual capability and for recognizing achievement, a system for granting credit for appropriate life experiences of their nontraditional students.

Academic advising. Many faculty members simply do not understand how nontraditional students differ from the traditional in their characteristics and needs. Faculty members' attempts at appropriate academic advisement often fall short of the mark. What is needed is intensive one-to-one academic counseling or small-group experiences in order to alleviate the new clientele's fears and insecurities when they first enter or reenter higher education. Quite often, the students cannot be on campus for the traditional academic advisement program. It is particularly difficult for part-time students to become involved in departmental activities, and thus they tend to become isolated and eventually are reluctant to seek out faculty members for academic advice.

Financial aid. For years, financial aid programs, both federal and state, have discriminated against nontraditional, part-time, and independent students. It appears the nation may now be revising its thinking and priorities to include them in financial aid plans. Further, colleges should adapt their internally funded financial aid programs to assure that nontraditional students are eligible for scholarships, loans, and grants. Otherwise, for many of these students, the increases in tuition are beyond their financial means.

Student services. Student service activities must be drastically adapted to meet the needs of the nontraditional students. Reentry programs should ease the transition to formal learning; counseling programs should address the special needs of older students—peer support, assertiveness training, and marriage counseling; practical problems are financial aid, child care, and car pooling; career planning and placement functions should be modified to help adult students reenter the job market.

Administrative support services. Administrative offices and services are generally geared to the schedule of traditional full-time day students and often are not available at times convenient for the nontraditional student. Administrative office hours will have to be extended into the evenings and the weekends. Members of the college's professional staff will have to be trained to deal with mature nontraditional students.

Curriculum. The curriculum must take into account the previous experiences of nontraditional students. They shouldn't have to learn what they already know. Courses need not be watered down or have the standards lowered, but they should be less teacher-centered and more learner-centered. Adult students want greater control over their conditions of learning. They do not, as Cross has noted, "come to school with a blank slate, waiting for it to be filled by teachers. They want to know how new knowledge relates to their own thoughts and experiences."[3]

Scheduling. We should begin to schedule *for* students rather than against them. Course schedules should be planned for the convenience of the students rather than for the comfort of the faculty members. Major courses must be rotated into the evening and weekends. Classes should be held at locations convenient to the students (but not necessarily to the faculty member whose office happens to be next door). Not all courses need be taught on the traditional semester or trimester basis. Small liberal arts colleges should consider the feasibility of offering short-term modules, mini-courses, internships, clinics, and other short, intensive programs.

Faculty Attitudes

For small liberal arts colleges to be successful in providing quality educational experience for nontraditional students, faculty attitudes must change. While the outside community may view

3. Ibid., p. 6.

faculty members as liberal and progressive, those who manage colleges realize that they may be liberal on certain national issues but are conservative about changing a curriculum or modifying the college mission. They, like many other social groups, feel threatened by change in the status quo. "Accustomed to the more select body of young adults who have reached higher education through the familiar path, . . . faculty seem to be obsessed with the fear that education geared to adults implies a lowering of academic standards."[4] Some of the fear is real and some of it is rhetoric. Part of the concern that many faculty members (and some administrators) feel is pragmatic. "It is relatively easy to make the case that in the past we have operated colleges for the convenience of teachers and administrators."[5]

If a small liberal arts college admits large numbers of nontraditional students, faculty members will have to adjust their life styles and teaching techniques. No longer will they be teaching the majority of their courses between 10:00 A.M. and 3:00 P.M. (with nothing later than 12:00 noon on Fridays). In order to maintain quality control, colleges will have to direct their full-time faculty members to teach in the evening and on weekends. If a college is to successfully enroll, educate, and retain large numbers of nontraditional students, it should prepare its faculty to serve the special needs of those students. A faculty development program will have to be established, and faculty members will need to be told in clear and direct language that the institution is modifying its mission and expects faculty members to modify their attitudes, teaching techniques, and life styles to respond to the needs of nontraditional students.

With some creativity and imagination, small liberal arts colleges can reduce the barriers to access and success. They can, as Greenberg of the Council for the Advancement of Experiential Learning stated at a meeting of the Association of Governing Boards, "provide small, personalized value-oriented communities for learners of all ages to return to again and again throughout their lives, as differing needs and life stages require. . . . they can add a dimension of quality to

4. Rosalind K. Loring, "Strategies of Adaptation," in *Adapting Institutions to the Adult Learner: Experiments in Progress*, Current Issues in Higher Education, 1978, no. 2 (Washington: American Association for Higher Education, 1978), p. 3.

5. Lloyd J. Averill, "The Effective College: Agenda for the 80's," *Liberal Education*, Spring 1980, p. 5.

persons' lives, increasingly difficult to find elsewhere."[6] Small liberal
arts colleges can successfully mix traditional and nontraditional
students as soon as they accept life-long learning as an important part
of their mission. Maehl has expressed the hope that our colleges will
"address the new mature students with the same integrity of mission
that we brought to our work with young people in the past. Above all,
we must not expect to exploit the adult learner just to preserve intact
what we have done in the past."[7]

The Changing Character of Small Institutions
Robert C. Maxson

Among the changes taking place in higher education in the last
decade, one of the most dramatic has been the nature of the student
bodies. Universities, both large and small, have experienced a striking shift from traditional students to what has become known as
nontraditional students.

The traditional student is stereotyped as being 18–22 years of
age, living in a dormitory, and displaying more interest in campus
life than in the academic program. The university community is
dominant in the students' lives. Their activities—recreational, social,
as well as academic—take place within the campus environment.
Many spend their weekends at the university, studying, working at
part-time jobs, or participating in social events sponsored by the
institution. This pattern has changed on many campuses—probably
on most campuses.

The nontraditional student is viewed by many as the "student of
the future." These students are characterized as being older and as
working and taking less than a full course load. With the nontraditional student comes a new set of demands and expectations. The
student is on campus only to attend classes and is not involved, and is
often disinterested, in extracurricular activities participated in by

6. Elinor Greenberg, "The Opportunity of a Lifetime," *AGB Reports*,
March/April 1980, p. 25.

7. William H. Maehl, Jr., "The Liberal Arts and the Lifelong Learner," *Liberal
Education*, Summer 1980, p. 192.

traditional students. Larger institutions cope with the traditional-nontraditional student mix by recognizing they have two distinct populations and simply provide programs, both academic and non-academic, tailored for the respective groups.

Pressures on Small Institutions

Smaller institutions may not have sufficient enrollments or resources to provide programs for two different student bodies. Thus, administrators on those campuses face unusual pressures in attempting to mix traditional and nontraditional students, pressures that come from many sources. Three major problem areas the administration faces in trying to meet the needs of both traditional and nontraditional students may be categorized as student life, academic programs, and faculty perceptions.

Student life programs. Traditional students perceive non-academic student programs—student life—to be entertainment-oriented. Dances, movies, athletics, and even artist-lecture series are regarded as recreational activities designed to provide relief from studies as well as personal enrichment. Health clinics and church-related student organizations act in loco parentis.

The nontraditional student views the student life arm of the university as a service organization. Fees to support athletics programs are, to them, less important than effective job placement services and computerized car-pooling programs. Most campuses operate student affairs as a self-supporting auxiliary enterprise. Thus, administrators of campuses with small enrollments and limited dollars generated by student fees find themselves having to make tough priority decisions about "student activities." Simply stated, should student affairs be entertainment-oriented, service-oriented, or both? The dilemma facing a university central administration may further be clouded by different needs on urban and nonurban campuses.

Academic programs. Historically, small institutions have had rather homogeneous student bodies. This characteristic has allowed the campus to design academic programs that respond to its students' needs, interests, and aspirations. New sets of needs and demands accompany the nontraditional student. They take the form of pressures for night classes, off-campus classes, and seminars conducted on an intensive basis—the antithesis of the requirement and preferences of the traditional student. These demands are, however, only logistical issues.

More difficult for the administrator is the question, What is the purpose of a college degree? Obviously, this query goes to the very heart of any academic issue. Nontraditional students are more career-oriented, and college degrees are perceived as a means to an end rather than ends in themselves. Older, working students have generally opted for vocational and technical curricula and the professional schools. An unfortunate corollary is their view that liberal arts are largely unnecessary for their career goals. As a result, pressure is exerted to reduce the number of courses required in the arts and sciences and to replace them with more "practical" job-related offerings. Again, the move is away from the traditional curriculum developed for the traditional student.

The move to make education more career-centered has led to debate among both faculty and administrators. What is an educated person? What does a college degree represent? Small campuses cannot afford to lose too many students; but how pragmatic should administrators become in attempting to satisfy the wishes of students? Before radical surgery is done on the traditional program, administrators and faculty should be alert to two generalities: on the one hand, a totally career-oriented curriculum may represent better preparation for the work world at the entry level. On the other hand, evidence indicates that persons who have solid backgrounds in the liberal arts and who possess strong verbal and written communication skills seem to function better at the higher levels of employment.

Perceptions of Faculty

Administrators may find that faculty are professionally at odds with the new clientele. Some senior faculty members find rewards and comfort in small institutions operating in a "mom and pop" fashion where students are close to faculty and there is much interaction, both in and outside class. Those faculty members could find their association with the new clientele is less satisfying because part-timers tend to be less interested and more removed—perhaps seem aloof. They certainly will not appear to be as reverent as students in the past.

Directions for Small Institutions

Americans value growth and bigness. It is easy for small institutions to suffer paranoia. They have, obviously, no athletics teams competing for national championships, no prestigious medical schools, and no famous law schools to which the small-campus administration can point with pride. Both persons and organizations want to make their own niche. Small institutions, in an effort to be different, often try to develop programs that are different from those of other institutions. Certainly, a creative and innovative curriculum not found elsewhere will set the institution apart from the crowd. Administrators will be wise to anticipate carefully the effects before undertaking such a radical change in institutional direction. Unique programs usually have high visibility but small enrollments. As small campuses face the certainty of scarce resources and the probability of declining enrollments, they cannot afford programs that are underenrolled.

Leaders of institutions enrolling three thousand or fewer students may be wise to stay with the traditional programs, but develop creative ways to deliver those programs to nontraditional students. Older persons learn differently from traditional college students and can assume more responsibility for their learning. Thus, faculty and administrators can develop exemplary programs, not in what is being taught but by the way in which it is taught.

II. ENVIRONMENTAL PRESSURES

NONINTELLECTUALISM

Rising Above or Getting Around the Barriers
Arend D. Lubbers

Those who are a part of the classical or liberal tradition of education regard development of the intellect as the foremost objective of the educational process. The mind that absorbs the richness of literature and language, that is imbued with appreciation for history and philosophy, and is immersed in the methods and language of mathematics and science, that mind improves its capacity to know and understand and, consequently, to explain, solve, and invent. Through study, research, and discourse, this process is carried on, leading to theories, theorems, and often proofs that change the understanding of life and the way people live. Learning for the sake of knowing is a commandment handed down by the god of the intellect. Nonintellectualism is anything on the campus that detracts from the process that helps the mind develop in capacity to think independently and creatively, to penetrate to the essence of a subject, and to understand broadly the traditions, values, and directions of one's own culture.

Sources of Nonintellectualism

In academe, there are always disagreements about what subjects or processes qualify as nonintellectual. The technological revolution spawned by original research of the highest intellectual level has created a society with a myriad of technical jobs. These jobs require sophisticated training. Colleges and universities have assumed responsibility for much of this training over the opposition or at the reluctant acceptance of liberal arts faculties. The practical application of highly intellectual research nurtured in the university, and the demands which that application makes on academe, are viewed by some as a threat to the perpetuation of the pure intellectual process itself.

In other words, the need for technical training has produced a demand for higher education from people whose chief goal in college is to prepare for a better job than they could otherwise get. To many intellectuals this goal of education is demeaning to the real purpose of the university community—the pursuit of knowledge and growth in intellectuality and consciousness. How purely intellectual the American campus was in its purest form can be debated. Nevertheless, the expansion of professional curricula has tended to reduce the emphasis on intellectual discourse and the pursuit of knowledge for its own sake, and instead has substituted a "how to" mentality, a training-for-a-job approach. To the intellectual, that direction of learning is a threat to high quality; to many taxpayers, who pay much of the bill for both public and private education, it is the reason for the university.

Throughout history the intellectuals of a society have been a small proportion of the population. A usual home for them was the university, and their thoughts, ideas, and endeavors gave the university its character. In the past thirty-five years in the United States, old colleges and universities and new ones have accommodated an avalanche of students. Higher education has experienced a kind of democratization in the sense that many citizens have participated in it. The question arises, Can 30, 40, or 50 percent of the citizens be intellectuals? Is that hope utopian or even desirable? Are the democratized university and the university as an intellectual center a contradiction in terms? Certainly the weight of numbers has put a strain on those resources in academia that help maintain a high-quality academic environment.

A recent force for anti-intellectualism on many a campus is the perilous financial condition of colleges and universities. When faculty and administrators are conferring and arguing about which programs to cut and which people to lay off, they are often preoccupied with personal survival, not the improvement of intellectual discourse. Although the economic problem varies among institutions and among states, a majority of the nation's colleges and universities face a financial crisis that saps energy and deadens the spirit.

For some time collective bargaining has been creeping into higher education. When a faculty organizes under collective bargaining, a whole new nonintellectual process enters the life of academe. Unfortunately, in many colleges, the industrial collective bargaining model appeared to represent the least time consuming or least expensive way to determine salaries and conditions of employment. It will take years for that process to work itself into the life of universities in a nondisruptive way. The dollar cost not only will never be regained but also will require a part of the budget that otherwise could be spent to improve academic quality.

Apparently our age is the age of entitlement. People believe they are entitled to more money, more power, more freedom to do as they please, less work, and less restraint. These ideas have permeated academia along with the rest of society. Now the entitlement is running into some hard economic facts. The socioeconomic problem may interest the intellectual for analysis and prescription, but when he or she is caught up in it personally, the problem consumes time and thought without bettering the quality of the university.

Financial problems, collective bargaining where it exists, and the political and public attention focused on the university appear to be taking more of the president's time and even the time of academic officers. When administrative leaders concentrate on money and politics at the expense of involvement in planning academic programs and participating in the intellectual discourse with faculty and students, the quality of the academic environment is impaired. It is nonintellectual when the leader of an academic institution has little time for intellectual leadership.

Good performance by the president and his staff in financial development and management and in politics aids the institution immeasurably. At the same time the work can be stimulating to those who do it. Also it is likely to be all-absorbing, and faculty members who want, appreciate, and are stimulated by intellectual leadership from the president, provost, and academic vice president are left disappointed at best, and at worst dulled.

Professional Schools and the Liberal Learning

To meet these forces of nonintellectualism, strategies must be devised. Though they may be difficult to implement, they must be tried lest institutions of higher education, with some exceptions, cease to be lively, intellectually fertile breeding grounds for ideas, solutions, and higher consciousness.

The largest segment of higher education cannot retreat from the growth of professional curricula. Not only are professional curricula here to stay in the university, but our society's future may depend on the university locus. Intellectuals in the liberal tradition of education must avoid dealing with their more professionally, even vocationally oriented colleagues as a threat to institutional mission, but, rather, find ways to make them part of the faculty intellectual fold.

Because the liberal arts curriculum has suffered while professional curricula have expanded, there are practical incentives for professors of the liberal arts to persuade, cooperate, and plan with their so-called more practical colleagues. If they live together, they can share credit-hour generation and student-faculty ratios.

A few years ago a decision was made at Grand Valley State to place the Schools of Public Service, Health Sciences, Nursing, and Education within the College of Arts and Sciences. This action was unpopular with many faculty members in Arts and Sciences and in the professional schools. The decision was made because the administrative leadership believed that all educated people need the perspective that comes from some understanding of the knowledge embodied by the liberal arts curriculum. The intellectual process that flows from liberal learning and the life of the mind was not negated or contaminated by the move. Rather, its advocates and purveyors were summoned to do what they claimed was necessary for high academic quality: require all students, even those in the professional schools, to spend a considerable time living with ideas and concepts more encompassing than those defined in one professional field. Structure was used to encourage dialogue and synthesis. Structure was used to bring together groups that usually prefer to go their own ways with little respect for one another. Both professional education and liberal education are important to the university enterprise, and if they are allowed to separate, they tend to bifurcate knowledge and the learning process.

How successful is the Grand Valley State plan to keep the growing emphasis on professional education firmly attached to and rooted in the intellectual tradition of liberal learning? The paraphernalia of academia are there. Faculty members from Arts and Sciences and the schools work together on committees, share in symposia, evaluate each other's curriculum, and see that all graduates of the schools have a good dose of liberal arts courses. Whether or not the structure has accomplished its major objectives of fusing the two groups into one intellectual community requires more time.

A complex modern society will have its highly trained specialists. The forward evolution of the human species requires intellectuals who work with values and with historical and personal understanding. They must live together in the university. The specialists need the intellectual generalists if the university community is to remain truly human and humane. The specialist will be here because knowledge has brought us a technological, specialized society that will not yield to intellectual Luddites.

Finances and Enrollments

Many colleges and universities played the numbers game in the 1960s and '70s. The temptation to increase enrollments in order to increase tuition income or to enable a college to qualify for higher appropriations helped bring legions of students to the campuses. Citizens wanted access to education and the promise of a better life, and the education empire builders accommodated them.

Before considering a strategy to counter nonintellectualism in colleges and universities, a first question is whether a large percentage of the population should be accommodated. There must be places where intellectuals pursue their work in the company of their own kind, unimpeded by large numbers of people. The nation has the faculty, plant, and wealth to educate in colleges and universities a significant proportion of its population. To do so, and do it well, is a noble objective. Our democracy in coming centuries will be more likely saved if more people are educated in the intellectual process. They will not all have high-quality intellects, but they can have historical, personal, and scientific perspectives that will help· them understand themselves, their society, and other societies more fully. If universities educate for jobs only, the result will be generations of disappointed people.

Rapid growth in higher education has ended for this century. Though fewer people will graduate from high schools, the same high proportion are likely to attend college. They will be accompanied by numerous older adults. No growth or a decline in enrollments for many universities does not mean the nation will educate only intellectual and economic elites. The most elitist professors and administrators may wish to provide college education only for a selected few, but that wish will not be realized in this country.

Universities now have an advantage not available when the enrollment pressures were great. The opportunity lies in faculty recruitment and development. In the steady or declining state of higher education, each college and university should have a plan for improving the quality of the faculty. Budget cuts are or will be a necessary exercise for most institutions, and they provide an opportunity to release the weakest teachers, researchers, and administrators. This radical move will strike the most impressive blow against nonintellectualism, and for a high-quality academic environment.

Faculty leadership must agree to the objectives of the plan, the board must support the president, provost, deans, and tenure committees, and all must make sure that the process is as just as possible as it works toward the objective. Early retirement, challenge to competence, removal of weakest programs, "buy out" can all be considered. In this difficult period probably the greatest opportunity for improvement in quality in most colleges and universities, particularly in the less well-known institutions, is in upgrading the quality of the faculty. The institution will be sued and the administration will be under severe pressure, perhaps in some cases beyond the breaking point. The quality of education will eventually improve by a 10–20 percent factor.

The financial crisis in higher education is caused by high inflation and recession. For some it is caused also by dwindling enrollments. The nonintellectual component of this crisis, as mentioned earlier, is the energy, time, and thought expended on campuses worrying about it, and fighting about what to do rather than tending primarily to the institutional mission, the intellectual development of students.

There is no strategy that can immediately calm a campus caught up in financial crisis. The strategy should try to bring the campus to some equilibrium within a few years. Instead of being overly concerned by the numbers problems, administrative and faculty leaders should decide who are the best people, what are their fields of study and research, what is the institution's natural clientele, and how the institution can be of greatest service. With those considerations in mind, a plan can be devised to shape the institution in a way that maintains the best quality for the projected number of students that the leadership believes can be sustained. The plan may call for a more rapid reduction in enrollments than would happen without a plan. This kind of planning requires decisions as tough as those necessary to meet each year's crisis. In the end, just perhaps the turmoil created may lead to greater stability in a few years.

Making Collective Bargaining Collective

To propose a strategy to combat the nonintellectualism brought on by collective bargaining taxes administrative creativity. No other process in the recent history of higher education is less conducive to creating an environment of high academic quality. The games that are played and the level of attack on individuals appear to be unworthy for people who are dedicated to the life of the mind.

Experts who disagree will be eagerly listened to by their colleagues as they explain their position.

Administrators in unionized colleges should bargain hard for the right to take steps to improve the quality of the faculty. With improved faculty and patient, just administrative leadership, militancy and pettiness may recede. If the local union leadership is wise and in charge, there is some chance for reasonable accommodation. Administrators should work for this kind of relationship. Where respectful communication occurs between local union leaders and the administration, a few significant agreements will permit education to proceed uninterrupted by posturing, anger, and disruption.

The best hope is that in time some of the adversarial characteristics of bargaining will decline as colleges and universities live with the process. Better professors will take the lead, and more experienced administrators will meet with them. In the end, less time, money, and energy will be spent in what is mostly a nonintellectual endeavor.

Financial troubles and collective bargaining, especially in tandem, are not conducive to furthering a trusting relationship between the president and the faculty. Yet, the best intellectual environment requires that the president give attention to the life of the mind at the university he or she serves. The president and the faculty must be engaged in intellectual discourse. Often a president must use special means to see that the faculty understands his or her commitment to their primary function. Faculty members may see the president as concerned only with finances and public relations. Though they may understand the need for attention to those matters, many also believe the president should be more prominent as a leader in matters of education. How the president conveys personal concern in educational affairs depends on individual style.

A suggested strategy for presidential and faculty involvement might include the following commitments from the president. (1) Reserve time for reading, study, and possibly research outside the field of university administration. (2) Encourage and accept invitations to lecture in a few classes a year. (3) When addressing the faculty on practical matters of finance and politics, relate the analysis to the educational purpose they serve. (4) Encourage and accept invitations from schools and departments to meet with their faculty members. (5) Invite small groups of the faculty to presidential discussion sessions on specific topics. (6) Be host to intellectual leaders from off campus, and invite faculty members to meet them. (7) No matter how large the campus, take time each month to walk through buildings and offices, visiting with faculty members about mutual educational concerns.

Each institution established and nurtured for the improvement of human beings appears to be continually vulnerable to forces, ideas, and perversities that threaten its usefulness and undermine its original purpose. The university is no exception. In academe, the changes that take place in our perceptions about life, and the conflicts and tensions born of those changes, are bad or good, depending usually on how we cope with them. Analyzed here are a few of the changes in American colleges and universities and how they may threaten the major purpose of higher education. Yet some ways are proposed through which these changes can be absorbed into the life of a university, not to the detriment of intellectual understanding and development, but to its continued ascendancy. In time, when a clearer judgment can be made about the issues discussed here, their outcome may be determined less by the degree of the correctness of the strategies proposed than by the spirit and values of the people in the university.

Should Education Be Useful?
David W. Ellis

"Nonintellectualism" as a topic leads immediately to questions that many of us in higher education have grappled with. What are the forms of nonintellectualism on our campuses today? Why has it surfaced at this particular time? And what should we do to address its effects on our students?

Nonintellectualism, as I perceive it, manifests itself in several ways. One example is the tendency among students to be overly interested in grades and the degree, at the expense of actual learning and growth. Even more worrisome is the excessive vocationalism as expressed by students' emphasis on a job after graduation as the only objective of education. The rising incidence of compromise in academic integrity—in blunt terms, cheating—is also part of nonintellectualism. Still further evidence appears in reports from campuses that students seem less interested in extracurricular cultural activities than were students ten or twenty years ago.

Last and perhaps of greatest concern is the common observation that students today seem less excited by the academic pursuit, less interested in learning for the sake of learning, less curious about understanding the material, and more concerned in simply being told what they have to know for the exam. Experiences will vary from campus to campus, but the general situation is sufficiently clear as to demand that we consider fully the causes of nonintellectualism in its various manifestations and search for solutions to stem its spread.

Some will see as causes the weakening of basic educational standards in our secondary and elementary schools. We all hear examples citing that students do not know the basic facts of history, geography, the cultural life of different eras, the development of science, and so on. This answer strikes me as being too simplistic: our own institutions take responsibility for having educated most of the teachers in the secondary and elementary schools, and I cannot believe they did so bad a job. I do believe there is some truth in the assertion that students are entering colleges with less broad and less thorough education than formerly. And I believe also that much of the immediate responsibility for nonintellectualism lies with the institutions of higher education and that we must confront the challenge squarely.

Broad, Integrated Education

All of us who deal with students have sometimes failed to make clear to them what in their learning will become useful to their lives. In *The Aims of Education*, Alfred North Whitehead makes two statements that address my concerns. He first writes: "A merely well-informed man is the most useless bore on God's earth." He then goes on to champion the useful education: "Pedants sneer at an education which is useful. But if education is not useful, what is it?"[1] Before pursuing these thoughts, I must define "useful." I do not use the term as meaning narrowly vocational "usefulness," with education being only a means to help the student obtain his or her first job, though this goal is important. I offer the basic premise that a varied and liberal education will be "useful" for the full expanse of an indi-

1. New York: The Free Press, 1967.

vidual's life and will serve that person in his or her diverse pursuits within a profession, the family, and society. Furthermore, I see much of the nonintellectualism described earlier resulting from students' inability to perceive the usefulness—the purpose—of much of what they are asked to study, except in an abstract, theoretical way.

To join these two points, I ask whether we may check the spread of nonintellectualism by moving to reestablish the proper sense of usefulness and purpose in our students' perception of their studies. My position is that our colleges and universities must restore to their courses, curricula, and teaching a much stronger commitment to the usefulness of education. I see two broad approaches to this challenge.

Applications of Higher Education

First, we who have responsibility for the educational mission must reexamine the relation of an academic major to the present and future life of the student as a well-rounded adult and as an effective member of society. Higher education has failed too often to convey the relationship between many of the nonprofessional majors in the arts and sciences and preparedness suitable to make choices among a wide spectrum of careers. Over the years, I fear, a mistaken belief has assumed that the major must lead directly to a profession or job in the way an engineering student moves into a position as an engineer. Students, whatever their disciplinary major, follow many different paths in life, both after graduation and later in life. The major, I think, should be seen as relating to the person's life as a whole and to the profession or job he or she chooses. Internships, work experience during summers, opportunities to experiment with different jobs after graduation all contribute to such linkages. During the college years both students and faculty members must pay more attention to the depth and variety of linkages from the major to other disciplines and to the issues which face both persons and the society.

Second, we must include attractive options in our general education courses so as to encourage students to explore the culture and discover the many applications of purposeful learning. Again I quote from Whitehead: "What we should aim at producing is men who possess both culture and expert knowledge in some special direction." Breadth of knowledge and experience are assumed to be fundamentally important for the well-educated man. We accept this belief without question but often fail to act on our commitment. Few teachers would deny the value of balancing depth and specialization with a broad general education. But how do we ensure a successful outcome? How do we impress students with the value of such a course of study and have them accept its relevance to their lives? How do we show that general education is something more than a collection of courses spread across different divisions and departments? For some areas of learning, these goals are best achieved through survey courses. My own feeling is that a wide variety of approaches may make sense, depending on the course, the philosophy of the institution, the level of development of the student, and, most important, the breadth and commitment of the professor. But courses and programs must be given significant useful content, clearly grasped by the student, both for immediate and for long-range personal development.

Three diverse examples will illustrate. First, as a chemistry professor, I note that many freshman chemistry textbooks include, frequently at the end, practical considerations of how chemistry is useful in understanding environmental issues, the properties of various plastics, or the structure and physical properties of large biological molecules such as DNA. But often the classes do not cover these sections or the student reaches them long after he or she has lost interest because the course failed to give a purposeful perspective to atomic theory or quantum mechanics or chemical bonding. With more attention to "useful" applications, the student can grasp these points not only as interesting, evolutionary steps in chemistry, but also as important tools for understanding the world we live in and how science contributes to it.

A second example could be taken from almost any discipline in the arts or humanities. Humanistic questions about meaning and value may have little appeal to the typical 18–22-year-old college student. But with age, these questions take on increased importance. A skillful teacher can introduce the student to ways of looking at himself or herself in relation to such matters. The courses on medical and business ethics, of great interest on many campuses, are one example of applying values students have gained in their learning.

Third, multiple ways of looking at issues that cut across disciplinary lines—energy, starvation, human rights, and so on—give the student a sense of purpose and usefulness of broad learning that is absent when addressed solely by one discipline.

In my view, we in colleges and universities have failed to provide our students adequately with the essential breadth and understanding of culture and the disciplines and of how they relate to students' lives. The potential is present for purposefulness and understanding in all the disciplines. By increasing the usefulness of what we teach in part by how we teach it, we can maintain a high-quality academic environment while inhibiting the nonintellectualism present on many campuses today.

If We Don't Know What We're Doing, We Won't Know What We've Done
Richard C. Giardina

Much—perhaps too much—ink has flowed on the subject of nonintellectualism on college campuses. Now an equal amount of ink is flowing on how to maintain a high-quality academic environment, undoubtedly in the face of nonintellectualism both on campus and off. If nonintellectualism and the pressures leading toward the dilution of academic quality are both realities, how can they be combatted? How can a university that supposedly espouses a strong liberal arts orientation maintain a high-quality academic environment in the face of countervailing pressures encouraging a dilution of quality?

In one sense, the answer is simple. You maintain academic standards by knowing where you stand. Or, to put it another way, when you know what you are doing, you will know what you have done. Here it might be asked: What does that mean? Where does the university stand? What *is* the purpose of a university that espouses a strong liberal arts orientation?

Curriculum and the Goals of Education

The major purpose of such an institution, in my view, is to develop students who will have attained, before graduation, the requisite level of general life skills and specialized expertise to enable them to perform effectively and fulfillingly in a complex, rapidly changing world. These goals are, of course, relatively easy to define but difficult to develop. They include such matters as logical, analytical, and critical thinking; an ability to communicate both orally and in writing; an ability to apply critical thought processes to new, varied, and often complex and ambiguous situations; a clear understanding of one's own values and the values of others and an ability to apply those values to solving problems and to making decisions; an ability to recognize the consequences of one value choice over another; and an ability to understand and manage the conflict that arises from different value choices made by people in daily human interactions.

The most appropriate way for an academic administrator to maintain a high-quality academic environment is to see, and to demand proof, that learning is taking place, learning that explicitly assures that appropriate skills, capabilities, and expertise are attained before the baccalaureate is conferred. Such an administrative role would include positive positions and steps to:

- Forge a consensus concerning the nature of the baccalaureate in relation to the type of individual the faculty wishes to see develop.
- Support—and defend against external threats—the maintenance of a quality faculty to implement the baccalaureate program agreed upon.
- Encourage continued rethinking of the curriculum to help students develop agreed-upon skills and expertise.
- Evaluate the efficacy of that curriculum in achieving student learning outcomes and faculty and student satisfaction.
- Clearly specify to incoming students what is expected of them, what capabilities they will develop if they follow a particular curricular path, and how they will know that these capabilities have been attained.

To this end, academic administrators must act as catalysts for meaningful innovation and ever-improving quality control; they must work *with* faculty and *through* faculty to push their own ideas and to support ideas of their faculty colleagues. We should not be afraid to go down some new and untried paths, constantly keeping in mind, however, that a university's curriculum is only as good as the faculty that teaches it. Ultimately, the faculty's commitment to a particular vision of the type of educated person it wishes to develop will be the best predictor of that vision's realization in the curriculum. Academic administrators would fail in their responsibilities if they did not attempt to harness that vision in productive—and perhaps unanticipated—ways and to keep everyone involved honestly pursuing that vision by constantly evaluating its fruits as exhibited in student learning.

The Role of General Education

A number of more specific comments regarding a liberal arts university are in order. Such an institution has a special obligation to serve persons from all socioeconomic backgrounds, in all walks of life, and of all ages. This duty dictates that adequate provision be made for what is now commonly called "lifelong learning." Such an institution must be responsive to the needs of the community and must attempt to provide programs to meet those needs. Nevertheless, it should not, like so many two-year colleges, attempt to be "all things to all people." It must remember that what people are willing to buy is only half of the equation. The other half concerns what the institution is willing to sell. The integrity of the university demands a clear commitment to the liberal tradition of higher education, with specialized programs springing logically and not artificially from that tradition. I have a number of concerns in this regard.

My first concern is for the quality of the curriculum and especially for the quality of the student learning that results from that curriculum. I firmly believe that general education is the thread by which the entire curriculum hangs together. I further believe that a student's general education must be defined as cultivating general life skills or basic human capabilities necessary to lead a productive and satisfying life in today's changing society. I am convinced that these skills and capabilities can be developed in a variety of learning contexts, both disciplinary and interdisciplinary and both within and outside the classroom.

If general education is the thread by which the entire curriculum hangs together, then the various areas of specialization are patches of cloth that make up the quilt. The faculty and administration of a university must have a clearly defined notion of what the quilt is to look like and how it is to be designed. If an institution's specialized programs are to have any relation to the liberal tradition of higher education, they must be constructed out of that liberal tradition. No specialized program must be permitted to exist if it rejects the importance of liberal education, consumes all the available units in a baccalaureate for its own purposes, or threatens to engulf other specializations on its way to dominance in the university. The baccalaureate major run rampant must be stopped. The basic purpose of the baccalaureate as a liberal and liberalizing degree must be reinstated to its once preeminent place. If this goal entails fighting battles with the specialized accrediting agencies, then so be it. These agencies must not be allowed to dictate how the institutions define and structure their baccalaureate degrees.

How are universities to prevent academic majors and accrediting agencies from running rampant? There is no answer other than long, hard, intensive, systematic, and purposeful academic planning. The curricular quilt must be a product of rational planning and design by faculty and administrative quiltmakers who know what they are about and what they are attempting to achieve, if the quilt is to have any chance of serving the purpose for which it has been fashioned. Planning, the allocation of resources based on that planning, and, if necessary, the termination of low-quality or inappropriate programs as a result of that planning are the only sure ways of maintaining control over the nature, direction, and thrust of the curriculum and over its academic quality.

Evaluation of Student Learning

My second concern—evaluation—stems from my concern for the quality of the curriculum. We, as faculty and academic administrators, must constantly be engaged in the process of assessing our successes and failures in fostering student learning. Systematic review and evaluation of our academic programs can bring us to a better understanding of the learning process and of how we can improve student learning through improved pedagogic techniques and better use alternative modes of presentation in the classroom. It can also help us consider whether our existing organizational and program structures are best suited to meet the needs that the faculty and the administration in consultation determine are important. Evaluation always assumes that education is a problematic concern and that it thus must be treated as an area constantly in need of reformulation and redesign.

Here one will be tempted to ask: Evaluation in relation to what? Education for what purpose? For its own sake? For entry into a career? For informed participation in society? For personal satisfaction and fulfillment? Surely for all these reasons; but here I have to admit that my own biases are especially evident. I believe that above all the other purposes it serves, a baccalaureate degree must first and foremost be a societally relevant degree, geared to developing learning pertinent to living in society as a liberally educated individual. We must be able to demonstrate to those who pay for the costs of higher education that we are producing graduates competent to assume useful and important roles in society and that we have the evaluative capability to measure their competence in ways that will be understood and accepted.

We must be careful here to define evaluation as being directly concerned with measuring student learning and competence. If we do not keep this primary purpose of evaluation constantly in mind, we may easily get caught up in what is essentially a nonintellectual focus on "accountability" defined by procedural issues such as control of spending, compliance with policies and rules, justification of existing or proposed programs solely on the basis of actual or projected enrollments, and nonproliferation of degree titles. "This preoccupation with procedural matters," according to Keith Warner and Kay Andersen, may well lead to actions that "prevent improvements of quality, or possibly even diminish quality."[1]

Ensuring Faculty Quality

My third and final concern is in regard to the people who are supposed to be assuring the quality of the curriculum and evaluating student learning—the faculty. It is important for academic administrators to work with the faculty to help bring more clearly into focus their own developmental concerns. Raising the quality of faculty performance within the instructional mission of an institution requires a faculty both committed to that mission and committed to a continual development of expertise in their own and related fields. Thus faculty research, retraining, and other developmental activities must be encouraged and supported, not only because of their intrinsic merit for an individual faculty member, but also because of their cumulative merit for the institution as a whole. This developmental concern thus follows hand in hand with a concern for curricular quality and for evaluation.

If the students are the heart of any institution, then the faculty and administration make up its head. It is necessary for that faculty and administration to keep its collective head if the institution is to continue to maintain academic standards and educational quality in a world in which standards and quality are measured according to

1. "Accreditation Influences on Senior Colleges and Universities in the Western Accrediting Region: Summary Progress Report and Interpretation," Prepared for the Western College Association and the Accrediting Commission for Senior Colleges and Universities, Western Association of Schools and Colleges, Oakland, California, December 1979.

"when the warranty runs out." The quality of student learning must have a warranty that does not run out before the life of the individual. The collective head of an institution must not be swayed by pressures and allurements that cause it to turn away from an explicit focus on those priorities that will assure the development in students of societally relevant and life-lasting knowledge, skills, and capabilities. Only if we know *what we are doing* to promote student learning and *why we are doing it* will we be able to know *how well we have succeeded* in accomplishing the task of maintaining academic quality.

Liberal Learning—Pressure to Reestablish Its Practical Value

Ralph Z. Sorenson

Senior managers often make pronouncements about the need for broad and liberal education among professionals generally and management leaders in particular. For example, David Rockefeller, board chairman of the Chase Manhattan Bank, has spoken about executive qualities:

> The chief executive in the year 2,000 will have to be more broadly gauged to deal with the delicate and divergent internal and external forces of the day. In addition to being a "generalist" in the very best sense of the word—with a feel for history, politics, literature, current events and the arts—he will have to be sensitive to public opinion and respectful of the public franchise over which he presides.[1]

Or again, Irving Shapiro, formerly chairman of the Du Pont Company, has said:

> If I were choosing a chief executive, I would not be overly concerned with his education or specific background. I would ask if he relates to the larger world or if he only knows how to produce widgets but can not do anything else.[2]

1. "The Chief Executive in the Year 2000," Speech in San Francisco, November 2, 1979.

2. "The Corporate Chiefs' New Class," Interview by Marshall Loeb, *Time*, April 14, 1980.

I think that the tenet as applied to the world of management education also holds true in the field of technical education, and Howard W. Johnson, of the Massachusetts Institute of Technology, has agreed. He said in his inaugural speech as president of that institution, in 1966:

> We hold that it would be inadequate for the basic education of the M.I.T. man to stop at science and engineering. We hold that both frameworks—science and the humanities—are complex requisites to the education of the man who is to occupy the leadership responsibility in tomorrow's world. The threat implied in the concept of separateness of the two cultures lies in the narrow arrogance of power based on assumptions of a preeminence of a specialty. This narrow specialization is what we propose to avoid. A specialization, I might add, found as easily in medical doctors, businessmen and politicians as in scientists and humanists.
>
> My point is that the future will demand of M.I.T. a great deal more than that it simply bridge the supposed schism between two cultures where the not so well rounded scientist can be as ignorant of Shakespeare as the humanist is of the second law of thermodynamics. We shall have to provide true generalists capable of dealing with the great problems cutting across every area of our lives.

Perhaps Sir Eric Ashby said it best back in 1958 in his essay "Technology and the Academics":

> A student who can weave his technology into the fabric of society can claim to have a liberal education; a student who cannot weave his technology into the fabric of society cannot claim even to be a good technologist.[3]

Thus the importance of liberally educated professionals does seem to be recognized by people at the top.

Before pursuing my discussion, let me give the setting for my advocacy of liberal learning. Babson College, the institution I head, has, as its principal mission, education for management. From that position, I declare that I am a believer in liberal education for at least two reasons. First, liberally educated professionals are, in my opinion, much more effective in doing their jobs. Second, liberal education contributes to making life more interesting, rich, and full.

Professional and—Not Versus—Liberal Studies

The problem of evaluating desirable qualities in professionals appears to lie less with top management than within organizations

3. *Technology and the Academics: Essays on Universities and the Scientific Revolution* (London: Macmillan; New York: St. Martin's, 1958).

and companies where the persons who actually do the hiring of young people—recruiting officers and some line and staff officers— typically place a much higher value on what they perceive to be practical and professional skills. They are likely to give greater weight to skills in accounting, finance, marketing, engineering, and computer science than to a grasp of history, politics, philosophy, literature, science, and the ability to think critically.

Frequently, students themselves, with an eye toward starting salaries and, to them, the practical realities of "getting a job," tend to give short shrift to the liberal arts and sciences. All too often, they consider these as medicine to be taken like castor oil, only under duress. This attitude is reinforced, in my own view, by starting salary differentials commanded by, say, accounting graduates as opposed to students of the humanities. The *Wall Street Journal*, on September 12, 1980, reported that the average liberal arts undergraduate who joined the work force in June 1980 was able to command a starting salary of $12,900. This figure compares with starting salaries for people with accounting degrees of $15,500; computer science, $18,700; people with electrical engineering backgrounds, $20,300. Those are major differentials, and students are simply being practical when they take such factors into consideration as they design their curricula.

The situation is not helped by various professional associations such as the American Assembly of Collegiate Schools of Business (AACSB), the accrediting body for business schools. The AACSB, in its accrediting standards, seems to say that the liberal arts should be studied principally (if not exclusively) in the first two years of college, with the final two years reserved for business subjects. This attitude has led to a dichotomous view of society—the practical professional world versus the world of the liberal arts and sciences.

I disagree with this view, for I believe a common thread runs through both these worlds. What is the thread? It is the ability to think critically and independently, the ability to identify and define problems, the ability to marshal and analyze evidence, the ability to reach independent conclusions, the ability to formulate solutions or recommendations, and the ability to implement these solutions and recommendations. These abilities are commonly referred to as the scientific method. An additional, vital thread that runs through the worlds of the professional and the humanist is the ability to articulate ideas and thoughts in a clear, persuasive fashion both orally and in writing. And finally, perhaps most important, is the ability, which both professionals and humanists need, to inject flair, humor, compassion, good values, and zest into all that they do.

Breaking the Barriers

All these things are important, regardless of what a person does with his or her life. Certainly they are important in the fields of business and management, as a few examples will indicate. A knowledge of the liberal arts and sciences is critical if employers are to create satisfying work environments for their employees; for this purpose, they must have an understanding of psychology and sociology. Building constructive relationships between business and government requires basic exposure to political science and some sense of the evolution of relationships between the private and the public sectors. Decisions about the design of new products, new factories, or new buildings ideally should be made with a keen eye for aesthetics as well as function. Involvement in multinational businesses today clearly makes knowledge of foreign languages, geopolitics, and cross-cultural relationships desirable. And certainly those who make decisions about sponsoring TV programs and designing advertising campaigns should be able to differentiate critically between good art and bad art, good literature and bad literature.

In some ways, our big problem may lie in the term "liberal arts" itself. The term is at best fuzzy and at worst downright misleading and misunderstood. Some people ascribe to it political overtones: the liberal leftist arts as opposed to the more conservative rightist professionalism. These are the kinds of people who refer to "pointy-headed intellectuals." Some people equate liberal education with nonuseful education, as opposed to professional or useful education.

And those in the other camp, in the "liberal arts camp," tend to speak pejoratively and patronizingly of narrow vocationalism as opposed to the only true education, which in their view is rooted in the liberal arts and sciences. For example, a press release of October 9, 1980, put out by the Commission on the Humanities, included the statement: "While the Commission recognizes the problem of liberal arts graduates in the job market, it nonetheless considers vocationalism a dangerous trend."

As long as there are people who believe that vocationalism is a dangerous trend, there will be a tendency to lash out against it, to fight it, and to end up with a two-world mentality. I once heard David Riesman of Harvard say that the mere fact that the liberal arts are called liberal arts is no guarantee that these arts, whatever they may be, will be taught in a liberal fashion. Nor is there any guarantee that the humanities will be taught in a humane fashion. By the same token, he suggested, there is no reason why vocational or professional skills cannot be taught in a liberating, humane way rather than in a confining, inhumane way. Put another way, those teaching the liberal arts are not immune from narrow-mindedness, just as those teaching vocational or professional skills are not by definition excluded from the fraternity of liberal thinkers.[4]

Through these opposing sets of prejudices, we in higher education have managed to get ourselves into a tremendous jam where, it seems to me, we are in two armed camps. By way of prescription and recommendation, I think the first move is to break down this armed-camp mentality. We need to destroy the notion that the liberal arts and the professions are at war with each other. Those in the liberal arts and sciences must get away from the idea that vocationalism is dangerous. Narrow vocationalism, yes, but vocationalism in and of itself, no. Those in the professions and business, by contrast, must shed the mentality that says that the liberal arts are a waste of time. What all of us really are seeking is liberally educated professionals, people who are skilled businessmen, engineers, doctors, lawyers and, at the same time, are full, richly compassionate beings. The two are entwined. Consequently, we in colleges and universities should become more willing to interweave curricula so that even in undergraduate programs at liberal arts colleges we recognize that the concerns for careers and the concerns for one's own future vocation are legitimate. Even though the major emphasis at the undergraduate level may be on the liberal arts and sciences, students need opportunities to get a feel for and exposure to different kinds of career paths. In turn, colleges like Babson that are primarily oriented toward management or professional education need, either through cross-registration or on their own campuses, increasingly to provide exposure for their students to subjects such as history and political science, literature, and languages, all of which go into the making of good managers.

In the world of business, chief executive officers must make sure that, in their organizations, the people who actually do the hiring will look for liberally educated professionals rather than narrow specialists with skills that have a short half-life. The chief executive officers

4. Remarks made at a colloquium on higher education, Wellesley College.

must, it seems to me, in the future serve more vividly as role models. They need to speak out articulately about the importance of the liberal arts.

For all of us, in higher education and in business, it is important to realize that education isn't something that takes place in younger years and ends with a college diploma or even a graduate degree. Rather, education is a continuing adventure throughout life. In the course of that adventure there are two integral halves to the whole. One half has to do with technical, professionally oriented skills, and the other half has to do with the liberal arts and all the other subjects that create a rich cultural background and at the same time cultivate better professionals.

Leon Botstein, president of Bard College, wrote pertinently in the *Chronicle of Higher Education*, July 9, 1979:

> The emasculation of the liberal arts stems as well from the idea that culture is an experience separate from the material conditions of life, from money, work, nationality, religion. It is considered an add-on, a dimension of leisure. The liberal arts have been relegated to the enrichment department of life and not to its core. That idea has bred the peculiar notion that vocationalism and the liberal arts are in conflict and that students' profound concern with how they are to make a living deserves reproach because it undercuts the argument for a liberal-arts education. This intense preoccupation with employment, with security, with practicality, is, on the contrary, a most encouraging and creative sign for a serious liberal-arts program. For it should force us to make the liberal arts more than cultural polish and develop them as an essential component of work and personal life, entirely compatible with the pursuit of self-interest in the workaday world.

I can't think of a better way to put it.

MEASURING INSTITUTIONAL RESULTS

Maintaining Academic Quality on the Cheap
Alexander W. Astin

Most institutions will find it difficult to respond effectively to "pressure to improve standards" as long as they continue to cling to traditional notions about "academic quality." I am among that small minority of educators who believe that academic quality is neither an elusive nor an ethereal concept. Two decades of research on this issue convinces me that there *is* considerable agreement among academics about what quality is. But unless these traditional definitions are replaced by more workable and, I believe, more valid conceptions of quality, most attempts to improve standards will fail.

Four Conceptions of Quality

Academics have traditionally favored two conceptions of quality, which I shall label the *reputational* and the *resource* conceptions. Taking the reputational approach, ask a group of educators to make quality rankings of institutions or, more simply, to name what they think are the "best" institutions. The answers will show an amazing degree of consensus about which the best institutions are. The resource approach equates academic quality with one or more of three types of resources: bright students, highly trained and prestigious faculty, and affluence (including, for instance, the institution's endowment, library, and physical plant). As it happens, those institutions with the greatest resources also tend to be the ones with the strongest reputations. In other words, reputational measures and resource measures are largely interchangeable.

A third definition of quality, which has become increasingly popular, is the *outcomes* approach, which equates quality with the proportion of entrants who eventually graduate, the earnings and other accomplishments of the institution's alumni, and similar assumed results—short or long term—of the educational process. Again, the quality rankings produced by outcome measures are very similar to those produced by reputational rankings and resource measures.

The fourth approach to quality assessment is what I call the *value-added* approach. This approach attempts to overcome some of the methodological limitations of simple outcome measurement by means of longitudinal data that compare student outcomes with the student's characteristics at the time of initial entry to college. The basic argument underlying the value-added approach is that true educational quality resides in the institution's ability to affect its students favorably, to make a positive difference in their intellectual and personal development. While I favor the value-added approach over the others, it has not caught on because institutions find that quality assessments of this kind are simply too costly and too time-consuming.

Among these four conceptions of quality, the resource approach has tended to dominate policy making and governance. This predominance is understandable, since tangible assets presumably can be increased through entrepreneurial leadership. Thus, academic administrators are usually rewarded for accumulating more bright students, more prestigious faculty members, and more money. Given the hierarchial nature of American higher education, this reward system seems to have a good deal of validity in that the most prestigious institutions at the top of hierarchy are also the ones that have the brightest students, the most prestigious faculty, and the greatest affluence.

Emphasis on resource acquisition may have served us well when American higher education was expanding rapidly and when the supplies of money and of students seemed limitless. The problem now, however, is that enrollments have stabilized and even declined and that public support to what has come to be a very costly system of higher education is declining as well. Under such conditions, there is no way for the higher education system as a whole to increase or even maintain standards based on acquisition. Educators must face the fact that the pool of student and faculty talent and available money is finite and that if we continue our mindless pursuit of these resources, not only will we fail in our efforts to raise quality and strengthen standards, but also we are likely to become chronically depressed.

If each of us sets aside his own institutional perspective for a moment and looks at the American higher education system as a whole, it becomes clear that this obsession with resource acquisition will not have much effect on the size of the total resource pool;

rather, it will result in little more than a redistribution of resources from the less successful to the more successful entrepreneurs. A more important point is that the time and energy currently being squandered in pursuit of resources could, in my judgment, be much more effectively used if they were focused on *how* to use the resources we currently have.

Facing Up to Contradictions

⌐I am convinced that higher education has the capacity to substantially strengthen academic standards and to raise the quality of educational programs with no additional resources and even with fewer resources, if necessary.⌐But first, our highly developed critical skills must be turned inward on ourselves. More specifically, it seems to me that the ways we currently use our resources are inconsistent and often contradictory. By understanding and facing up to these contradictions, we can substantially improve our programs.

Devaluation of Teaching

I shall cite a few of these contradictions and suggest how they might be resolved. The first contradiction involves our old friend, research versus teaching. While this issue has not been at the top of priority lists in recent years, and while some may even think that it has been solved, mere claims that research enhances teaching or that research and teaching are valued equally are not consistent with the facts. Most college teachers are trained in graduate departments that concentrate practically all their resources on the development of research skills; little or no attention is given to the development of teaching skills. Once the new doctorate recipient lands an academic job, the pattern continues: Faculty members continue to develop research expertise by means of publications that are regularly reviewed by peers, but few faculty members receive systematic peer review of their teaching performance.

The increased use of student evaluations of teaching is, to be sure, a positive sign, but such ratings are typically used to reward and punish teachers rather than to provide feedback that will facilitate the development of their pedagogical skills. Further, in most institutions, classroom visitations by peers, videotaped classroom sessions, and other methods that could serve to develop teaching are still used only sporadically, if at all.

False Claims

A second contradiction in academe lies in the claim that colleges and universities are *educational* institutions dedicated to student learning and development. Actually, one can identify a whole set of contradictions related to this claim. Let me start with administrative practice. Reading through the typical treatise on college administration or management, one is hard put to find any reference to student learning and development. Indeed, the so-called management information systems that have become increasingly popular in recent years are replete with data on budgets, enrollments, course loads, and physical plant and facilities, but say practically nothing about the educational progress or development of students. In effect, college administrators are encouraged to plan and make decisions without regard to what is happening to students. To me, this omission is analogous to trying to run a commercial business or industry without any information on sales volume, profits, or losses. In other words, the "business" of academe is not budgets and endowments and enrollments, but rather the enhancement of student learning and development. Unfortunately, our current approaches to management do not encourage administrators to think in such terms.

We claim that our colleges and universities are educational institutions, and yet we continually disregard many of the basic principles established in literally thousands of studies of human learning: such principles as knowledge of results, immediate feedback, and vigilance or "time on task." This last principle states that the amount of learning that takes place is directly related to the amount of effort that the student puts out. It is a serious mistake to assume—as educators have done in recent years—that students will benefit if the undergraduate experience is made as easy and as painless as possible. As a matter of fact, evidence suggests that students are more, rather than less, likely to drop out when they are not challenged.

We claim that we are interested in what happens to our students, and yet we seldom survey student opinion and even more rarely conduct surveys of our dropouts and our alumni except when accreditation time comes around. If we really care about the quality of our educational programs, such surveys would be a routine part of our institutional practice.

We claim to be concerned about the education and development of all of our students, and yet we continue to insist on using admissions and grading practices that are meritocratic and normative., Thus, we admit only the "best" students, thereby excluding those who might be in the greatest need of further education.]Those underprepared students who are admitted are usually channeled into community colleges. Given that the facilities, educational climates, and funding levels of community colleges are generally less desirable than those of universities, such an institutional arrangement serves to deny an equal educational opportunity to poor and minority students, who tend to be disproportionately concentrated in community colleges.

Even after students are admitted, our meritocratic grading system limits what we can do educationally because it presupposes that there will be "winners" and "losers." Not everyone can succeed in such a system, and one person's achievement is another person's failure. The obvious problem here is that our grading practices deny the fact that *all* students are capable of learning and that one student should not be penalized if another learns more or at a faster rate. There is simply no reason why this meritocratic grading system cannot be replaced with a system that measures whether, and by how much, each student learns and develops, without comparison with other students.

Denigration of Education

But perhaps the most subtle contradiction concerns how we in the academy view education. We claim to be educational institutions, and yet the very field that should have the highest status within the academy—education—actually has the lowest status. The patronizing attitude of academics toward education is reflected in a variety of ways. Twenty-five years ago there were more than two hundred teachers colleges in the United States; today there are practically none. Virtually none of our most elite institutions offers an undergraduate major in education. Bright students who want to become schoolteachers are frequently encouraged to switch into some other, more "demanding" field. Thus, it is unsurprising that, of all the undergraduate majors, education has the most poorly prepared students at the entering freshman level. We in the more lofty reaches of the education system are fond of criticizing the secondary schools, but could it be that the chickens are coming home to roost? that the declining educational competences of today's freshmen are directly attributable to the poor quality of the teachers that we sent out to educate them?

In short, these contradictions convince me that our claim that we are dedicating our resources to educating our students is not supported by many of our time-honored practices and policies in admissions, grading, faculty training, faculty evaluation, information collection and dissemination, and administrative practice. If one accepts the view that the ultimate test of an institution's quality is how well and how much its students learn and develop, then it seems clear that *American higher education has enormous undeveloped potential in its existing resources.*

An Encouraging Irony

These contradictions add up to an encouraging irony: Focusing our existing resources more directly on the education of students may be the best way to guarantee that resources will be sufficient in the future. I suggest that current public cynicism and negativism about higher education may be in part our own doing. The condescending attitudes of academics toward the art and profession of teaching have not gone unnoticed by the students who have passed through our institutions over the past several decades. Many of our voting citizens, and practically all of our politicians and policy makers, have been exposed to four or more years of higher education and have almost certainly acquired some of their professors' attitudes about education. If the next generation of college students is exposed to a different kind of experience—one where teaching, learning, and education are valued rather than denigrated—then public support for higher education is almost certain to increase.

Outcomes Information— A Way to Assert Leadership

Dennis P. Jones

Information about the outcomes of higher education, particularly student outcomes, seldom is regularly collected and made available to institutional executives. Inasmuch as improved institutional strength is an important outcome of an institution's activities over time, much information about programs, faculty, finances, and other resources can legitimately be regarded as outcomes information. But this kind of information almost never is generated primarily to gauge outcomes and seldom is recognized as having that significance.

Alexander Astin observes that most institutional information systems contain nothing but the most simplistic student and outcomes information. He concludes that the "benefits" (outcomes) side of the decision equation is generally ignored because information systems are inordinately oriented toward resource information.[1] An alternative explanation is that neither the ongoing operations of colleges and universities nor the needs of institutional decision makers have created a demand for readily available information on outcomes.

There are signs, and some evidence, that this situation is changing. As with most significant organizational changes, the pressures for change are generated, directly or indirectly, by conditions in the external environment. In an increasingly competitive environment, institutions find that it pays to do some things particularly well; competition creates incentives for quality and effectiveness as well as for efficiency. Some of the new interest in measures of outcomes and quality represents a strategic response by institutions to the strictures inherent in funding formulas, most of which historically have been keyed to *quantity*—to numbers of students and faculty and volumes of activities.

In other instances, outcomes information is being externally mandated. Some states are experimenting with funding formulas and other resource-allocation procedures that recognize achievement of outcome objectives or improvement of quality through the development of centers of excellence. Indeed, outcomes information may be a condition for funding, an example being the requirement that institutions receiving federal vocational-education funds obtain specified information from graduates through follow-up surveys. This rising interest in outcomes information, as both a philosophic and practical necessity, forces attention on the fact that the outcomes components of information systems at most colleges and universities remain relatively undeveloped. The requisite development will involve more than technical expertise, and decision makers will be ill-advised to ignore the issue.

1. "Student-Oriented Management: A Proposal for Change," in *Evaluating Educational Quality: A Conference Summary* (Washington: Council on Postsecondary Accreditation, 1979), p. 3.

The Architecture of Outcomes Information—
Let Form Follow Function

A great diversity of potential outcomes may result as the collective or individual consequence of educational experiences in an institution. Oscar Lenning developed at the National Center for Higher Education Management Systems a list of such outcomes, largely through synthesizing knowledge derived from research on outcomes measurement and from literature on the goals and purposes of postsecondary education.[2] The list is impressive, spanning economic and occupational outcomes, aspirations, competences and skills, affective and perceptual characteristics, the social benefits of an educated citizenry, and more. No institution seeks to achieve all these potential outcomes fully; each must be content with patterns of emphasis. At some institutions the mission is to train persons for certain occupational or professional pursuits. Other institutions seek to develop the educated person. Still others wish mainly to inculcate or buttress certain religious values and beliefs. What information on outcomes is most important to a given institution depends on the institution's purpose, which, in turn, reflects its values.

This observation is critical, because most institutions start their systematic collection of outcomes information virtually from scratch. Since little outcomes information is readily available from ongoing processes at the institution, the tendency to rely on what is available, rather than on what is needed, is largely offset. This circumstance offers uncommon opportunity and encouragement to start right. It is best to begin by identifying the kinds of outcomes about which some information is most important, even if there is doubt about whether precise information about those outcomes can be acquired. In the end, it is better to have inadequate information about the right things than to have precise information about the wrong things.

The Measurement Issue: *How* as Well as *What*

Deciding *how* outcomes are to be measured, identifying what evidence is to be compiled about selected outcomes, may be as important as the initial selection of priority outcomes, for two reasons. First, approaches to measurement involve concrete representation of more abstractly stated missions, purposes, and consequences. Purists may argue that information is value-free, yet

2. *Outcomes Structure: An Overview and Procedures for Applying It in Postsecondary Institutions* (Boulder, Colo.: NCHEMS, 1977).

selecting the ways outcomes are to be measured is still an exercise in stating values. Consider how easy it is to agree in the abstract that institutions should be effective and productive, yet vehemently disagree with those whose values demand that effectiveness be measured in cost per credit hour. To cite a subtler instance, consider the different values and assumptions reflected in a decision to measure academic preparation by ascertaining *how many* of an institution's graduates proceed to graduate programs without considering *which* graduate schools or with what measure of success.

Second, the measurements selected largely determine the credibility and usefulness of information, to both internal and external audiences. Information must not only be valid, but also be perceived as valid by those who are to use it or be persuaded by it. In short, *how* an abstract concept such as occupational preparedness is measured has much to do with the usefulness of information to different audiences. Some research results indicate that different audiences have different preferences with regard to evidence.[3] For example, internal groups are more likely to accept grades and test scores as evidence of occupational preparation than are external groups, which are more interested in information about job placement or satisfactory work performance. Measurement approaches selected should reflect established user preferences; if this criterion is not feasible, pains must be taken to win acceptance of the measures chosen.

Semantic Hurdles: Quantitative, Qualitative, MIS

Semantic and conceptual problems swirl around the terms *quantitative information* and *qualitative information* and the images associated with *management information system* (MIS). The language problem obscures what is important in considering educational outcomes and information about those outcomes. "Quantitative" becomes synonymous with *objective, factual, simplistic,* and *unimportant* (if you can measure it, it can't be important). In word-association games, *qualitative* more often than not will be taken to mean *subjective, value-laden, difficult,* and therefore closer to the core of what higher education is all about. Mention *management information systems,* and quantitative information and computer technology are immediately brought to mind.

3. Sidney S. Micek and William Ray Arney, *The Higher Education Outcome Measures Identification Study: A Descriptive Summary* (Boulder, Colo.: NCHEMS at Western Interstate Commission for Higher Education, 1974).

When the semantic underbrush is cut through, however, it becomes clear that the main issue is not quantitative versus qualitative, but measurement itself—the gathering of evidence that can indicate the (relative or absolute) level or presence of a particular consequence or condition. Measurement can take many forms, from pure counting (usually called "quantitative") to quantitative representations of subjective judgments (voting or assigning a 4.0 to an essay) to nonquantitative expression of outcomes (services rated good or bad).

Similarly, to identify MIS as synonymous with technology is subverting. An MIS might better be thought of as any means of systematically acquiring and holding information important for informing management decisions or shaping the intentions and goals of executives. A regularly used clipping service fits this definition as well as the stereotypical computerized MIS does.

The overriding issue should not be the technology. Rather, the primary concern should be that the information be acquired often enough (perhaps every three to five years) to provide an acceptably accurate reflection of reality and to be credible. Collecting information through personal communication with community leaders is a legitimate form of MIS so long as the information is relevant, reasonable, trustworthy, and periodically updated.

Implications for Leadership

Three general implications for institutional executives derive from the points made.

1. *Take the initiative in identifying information needs.* At root, outcomes information is a means for articulating and communicating institutional values. The selection of what is important is not a technical task, but a leadership task. Outcomes information is a tool that can be used to shape both institutional direction and the image of the institution held by various constituents. Avoiding involvement in the process amounts to abandoning an opportunity to make an institutional statement, with these alternative results: (*a*) no statement gets made, (*b*) a statement gets made, for better or for worse, by someone else within the institution, or (*c*) the institution must accept an externally developed interpretation of outcomes and associated values (as happened when the Vocational Education Data System operationally defined vocational preparation in a particular way). Involvement extends beyond identifying *what* to measure to include concern with *how* to measure.

Top-level initiative is important both economically and substantively. Developing an information resource is, essentially, an investment decision, involving both initial costs and operating and maintenance costs. The list of potential outcomes measures is extremely long. NCHEMS has identified 400, without beginning to exhaust possibilities. Since adoption and use of any one measure can be costly, institutions simply cannot afford an undirected approach to selection and collection of such information.

2. *Take a broad view of information and systems for acquiring and storing it.* In selecting approaches to measuring outcomes, give priority to identifying phenomena to be described and look broadly for ways to acquire evidence. Pay particular attention to the way desirable values are reflected in the measure, and assess the credibility of those measures vis-à-vis important audiences. Let measurement technology be the servant of the process, not its master.

3. *Seek consensus about outcomes measures.* Leadership initiative in establishing institutional purpose and standards of excellence does not end with the selection of measures that reflect those values. It extends to using the tool for institutional betterment and improvement of external understanding. Thus internal decisions should reinforce a commitment to the selected purposes and standards. Perhaps more important, efforts should be made to gain constituent acceptance of the purposes and standards that inhere in the concrete form of outcomes measures.

Quantity versus Quality in Academic Planning
Paul J. Olscamp

Practices that have far-reaching adverse consequences have arisen from the misuse of quantitatively based accountability systems in higher education. Of these practices, the worst is to do academic planning on the basis of such systems. The effects have been disastrous. Nonetheless, those who engage in planning for academic programs, such as faculty members and academic administrators, must be able to provide a rationale for program development, and if the basis is not quantitative, then they must be able to say what it is and how well they do it.

Pressures for financial accountability, formulated so that comparisons among institutions and, later, states could be made, became acute in the early 1960s. The pressures arose when attention was drawn to the gap between the huge amounts being spent in higher education by the states and the federal government, and the relative absence of spending controls. Subsequently, cost analysis techniques were developed by, among others, the National Center for Higher Education Management Systems, the National Association of College and University Business Officers, the staffs of state coordinating and governing boards, and federal auditing agencies.

As the auditing technology spread, bureaucratic pressures led to greater uniformity among the instruments until the basic parts of the accountability system were nearly universal across the nation. The most used concepts were:

- SCH (student credit hour or hours)
- FTE student (full-time equivalent student)
- weighted and unweighted class size ratios
- FTE faculty position (again, full-time equivalent)

Support devices for distributing costs—the NCHEMS, ICLM (induced course load matrix), and similar models—were developed, and formulas were set in place, using the four basic numbers as drivers, and operating from an initially more or less arbitrarily chosen set of basic operating cost numbers, such as "X dollars per FTE faculty position per course level," "X dollars per net assignable square foot of program space," and "X dollars per FTE student for support services." Soon, almost everywhere in the public system, and at many places in the private sector, equipment, operating and capital budgets, as well as faculty and support staff positions were tied to these formulas.

Limitations of Cost Analysis Techniques for Academic Planning

Today, annual budgets are negotiated with most state legislatures almost entirely as a question of increasing or decreasing the various formula levels. All these developments have taken place within about twenty years. Some facts about the system should be noticed. (1) Numbers can produce only other numbers as products. (2) The ratios between SCH generated and program size have never been proportionate; that is, some programs have always been parasitic on others, largely because they were parasitic when this system was instituted. (3) The pressure on proposed *new* programs to generate some particular ratio of SCH to FTE faculty positions is much greater than the pressures on older, established programs. A supposed demonstration of the ability to produce such a ratio is a typical sine qua non for an agency or board recommendation of a new program. (4) Programs with heavy student demand use their SCH production as the chief internal argument for net additional resources. (5) In recent court decisions involving financial exigency, the accepted corroborating evidence for termination of programs, that is, jobs, has rested largely on historical and comparative SCH production. And, finally, faculties understand all of this very, very well.

What are the results for academic planning? They include at least the following points.

These numbers, these numerical descriptions, have become the central *prescriptors* in state-level planning and funding for public higher education. They are, of course, educationally irrelevant; they tell us what enrollments, staffing levels, and costs are or may be at a given moment in time, and that is all. Only one or two states (Tennessee is an example) have made any efforts to plan and budget even partially on a qualitative basis.

Because pressures at the state level have been great and institutions have responded by developing program presentations in the numerical format, internal program requests now also frequently use this format, indeed, often are required to do so.

Most important, almost every institution stipulates an established body of required courses, which are, therefore, fully enrolled and thus generate SCH. The resulting SCH in turn support other relatively underenrolled courses; that is, they produce faculty jobs to teach those courses. Thereafter it is virtually impossible to alter the required course pattern unless overall enrollments are rising at a rate that will generate more new positions under the formula than would be jeopardized by removing the required courses or by making them elective. Inasmuch as most general education courses are required, institutional planners, be they academic administrators or faculty planning committees, are stuck with them for so long as the departmental faculty controls the curriculum—as it should. The general faculty cannot be expected to commit hara-kiri for the sake of the program. Add to this rigidity the legal requirements for program closure and consequent termination of tenured faculty positions, and what follows is truly a situation in which no managerial skills are really relevant.

Where previously required courses have become elective and the proportion of faculty under tenure is high, morale is terrible. This situation holds even when the subject matter is essential to the production of educated persons, the classic case being foreign languages.

It is ironic in the extreme that one stated purpose that the early statewide accountability systems were to serve was to give institutions more, not less, flexibility in the curriculum. The idea was that the more precise the information about enrollment demand, the faster institutions could respond by changing their programs. But when that very same information is used as a funding base, it threatens the jobs of faculty members already on the scene, and the planners in fact have less, not more, flexibility.

Criteria for Academic Planning

Philosophers have known for millennia that normative conclusions cannot be generated from descriptive premises. Educational principles are normative; numerical analyses and projections are descriptive. It's impossible to get from one to the other unless it is assumed that what is and what ought to be are the same, in which case any academic planning is vacuous. Because numbers are understandable by everyone, the difficult part has been passed over, that is, the question of what we should do to *educate* people, not merely produce SCH. These are *two* things, not one. As soon as it is perceived that they are two things, the necessity to develop criteria for academic planning that are not numerically based is obvious and clear. It is possible to develop appropriate criteria for academic planning and to justify them. I would like to suggest how. This argument does not imply that accountability of the numerical sort has no place; on the contrary, it has the place it originally had—financial accountability.

Theoretically, academic planning for professional schools presents no great problems. Entrance can be by competitive examination; the number of places available can be determined by market analysis of need; and outcomes testing of skills and competences are, in principle, not difficult. In part, the lack of difficulty lies in the specificity and particularity of the skills taught and tested in professional schools. Anatomy, torts, and materials stress are fairly straightforward. The professional school does not try so much to produce *kinds of people* as it tries to produce people with certain skills and knowledge.

The Purposes of Liberal Education

Professional education as an example is informative to our purposes. Because general and liberal education *is* concerned with the kinds of people leaving the program, its primary emphasis is *not*, or should not be, the imparting of particular knowledge and specialized skills, but the production of *universally* applicable and *universally* valued personal characteristics. I suggest that no person in any society is truly educated unless he or she possesses most of the following characteristics. I also believe that one can tell by various means whether these characteristics are present or absent. What are the characteristics or qualities in question? There are many, and I shall suggest but a few.

- The ability to analyze and to synthesize, that is, to break complex wholes into their simplest parts; then, having recognized the relationships that explain the parts, to recombine them in accordance with these relationships, whether they be causal laws, means to ends, logical implications, or mathematical necessities;
- The ability to sift and weigh evidence, and assign appropriate degrees of relevance and importance on that basis;
- Reflectiveness, or the ability to consider things in terms of their consequences, without preconception, and with a willingness to surrender belief should the consequences imply that need, and the capacity to think impersonally;
- The ability to distinguish between fact and value, and to see that values are more important than facts. As Brand Blanshard notes, all of the machinery of the world (including educational institutions) serves persons, and is ultimately justified by its contribution to persons' abilities to enjoy intrinsic values, such as comfort, rest, richness of mind, a sense of freedom and dignity, and the satisfaction of curiosity;
- The ability to appreciate beauty, and to articulate and defend one's aesthetic choices;
- The ability to speak well, with some style as well as a mastery of one's subject;
- The capacity to appreciate the value of diversity and the toleration attendant upon this appreciation;
- Some subtlety of humor;
- Perseverance and discipline in one's problem solving;
- Heightened curiosity in the presence of the unknown or the ill-understood;
- The ability to control the fear that is based on ignorance;
- An awareness of right and wrong, and the capacity to defend and explain one's moral beliefs.[1]

---

1. In the preceding points, readers will note my indebtedness to Brand Blanshard, *The Uses of a Liberal Education and Other Talks to Students* (La Salle, Ill.: Open Court, 1973).

These are only a few of the qualities that differentiate the educated person from those less fortunate. The list would also include some properties that are not universal in character, but are particular to one's society or some set of societies, such as "Western society" or "the English-speaking peoples." Thus, the definition of "educated person" will vary in time and place, and will always be subject to some disagreement and to continual change. But without such a concept, there would be no reason for the existence of our institutions other than for technical and professional education.

People can, of course, be educated in settings other than college. In our society, however, college is the easiest and most convenient place for bringing these qualities to fruition, especially in the young. I do not claim that any particular, set curriculum will produce these attributes in our students, and, further, if the students do not have the requisite native abilities, no curriculum will achieve the goal. Experience has shown that certain disciplines are effective in this role and might be referred to as the "core curriculum." They include, but are not limited to, literature, history, philosophy, mathematics, physics, and selected other additions from the arts and sciences. Clearly, we must argue that teaching and learning such a curriculum is causally related to certain qualities in our graduates, or profess to the absurd position of saying either that they have none of the qualities I have enumerated or that we are in no way responsible for the presence of the qualities. In the former case no college graduates would be educated, and in the latter we would not be responsible if the qualities were present. In either case, the colleges would be useless. The test then is to show two things: that our graduates do have the qualities that classify them as educated, and that the work of the faculty with the curriculum contributed to the presence of the qualities.

It is in this sense of "quality" that I refer to "qualitatively based" academic planning, that is, a curriculum and a set of educational activities designed to produce qualities in persons that define them as educated. *Excellence* is concerned with how *well* colleges do this, and is a comparative concept.

Testing the Quality of Education

"Outcomes testing" as a concept seems to me to contain little that is new. I think I have been testing outcomes for years as a philosophy professor, and, indeed, if what came out wasn't what I wanted, the student stayed where he was. Call it what you will—competence testing, outcomes measurement, or final examinations—the concept is the same. That is, presumably, we, both as academic planners and faculty members, have been trying to impart certain skills, develop certain capacities or dispositions, instill certain values, and impart certain attitudes to people who did not have those qualities and aptitudes, or did not have them to the same degree, before we did our work. The mechanism for ascertaining the level of our success or failure has always been, and still is, some sort of test. As educational institutions, we have, quite simply, not been very thorough. What we should have been doing all along is testing students when they first arrive for the presence or absence of the *same* attributes for which we intend to test them when they graduate, after the faculty members have done their work. After similar testing at graduation, the differences should be analyzed. If there are significant differences, they are obviously owed to something that happened between the tests. The testing instruments can be designed to demonstrate that "something" to which the difference is owed is the instruction, example, and practice provided by the faculty in the interim. The instruments clearly cannot be discipline specific in tests for the kinds of qualities I have listed here. They would have to be oriented toward capacities or abilities rather than primarily toward specific content. But they also require content, the demonstration of factual knowledge, in the proving of the capacities. Several attempts to develop such tests are under way, the best known of which is probably the COMP battery (the College Outcome Measures Project of the American College Testing Program).

The final step in the process is the one with the bite! If we manage to do what has been suggested so far, we would be able to show that we had made the difference we wanted to make, and said we would make, in a person's life. That is, we would be able to justify our institutional effort educationally. But this result alone would not tell us how well we educate, at least not completely. For that, we would need to know how well we stack up against other institutions that are trying to do the same thing. And this step suggests to me the use of *standardized* tests for similar institutions.

In weighing quantity versus quality in academic planning, the following conclusions and suggestions emerge.

Quantitatively based accountability is suitable for cost analyses and verification and for describing the present state of an institution in numerical terms. It cannot provide either standards for education or verification that we are educating students. Thus, it cannot be the basis of academic planning.

Educational or academic planning should be based on an understanding of what kinds of qualities and attributes collectively define an educated person.

A sound curriculum is planned to produce such qualities.

Educational justification at the institutional level, as opposed to quantitative accountability, now becomes a matter of testing to see whether a given curriculum and faculty have in fact produced educated persons. Both entrance and exit tests are required.

Knowledge of institutional educational *excellence* could be gained by using standardized tests to compare graduates of institutions of the same kind.

Finally, I suggest that, at least internally, the basis for the allocation of resources should be the educated person planning model. I further suggest that public college administrators would be in a far better position to persuade legislators to fund our institutions adequately if they could prove to the legislators that our colleges produce educated persons. At present, there is no easy way to do so.

III. MANAGEMENT PRESSURES

ADMINISTRATIVE TALENT

"Management" of Higher Education—
A Skeptical Comment
Howard R. Bowen

What do we mean by "modern management techniques"? To me, they imply concepts such as market research, operations research, cost effectiveness, systems analysis, program budgeting, management by objectives, long-range projection models, marginal cost analysis, accountability, and so on. Most of these techniques conjure up quantification and computerization. It is widely believed that they are highly effective in business management and that they would be equally applicable and productive in higher education. Some enthusiasts even argue that the financial problems of higher education would be resolved if only "sound, hard-headed, rational" business management procedures were adopted.

I have deep skepticism about the applicability of the tools and the spirit of business management to higher education. I find even the semantic overtones of the word "management" objectionable when applied to colleges and universities, and much prefer the less provocative "administration." Institutions of higher education are, or should be, concerned with the personal development of individual human beings and the advancement of the culture, and these are not readily quantified.

I have often asked myself what percentage of the budget of my own institution would be trimmed by adopting one or more of the newer management devices. My answer has always come out the same, "precious little." Real cuts would come, not from systems analysis or program budgeting, but from the *judgment* that some activity was not producing outcomes worthy of the cost and from the *leadership* that would bring about the change. Indeed, I am not sure that the slick tools of modern management have succeeded even in business. In recent years, just as the very height of management in this sense has been attained, the industrial productivity of the nation has stopped growing. Moreover, as every consumer knows, part of the much-vaunted progress of the American private economy has been in the form of quality deterioration and curtailment of consumer services. But even conceding that the new management techniques have helped business, it does not follow that they would be equally applicable to human services in the nonprofit sector.

I define true administration as the use of judgment and leadership in the quest for efficiency. Efficiency, as economists understand it, is not the same as cost cutting. Efficiency is a ratio between two variables: cost and benefits. Efficiency can be improved either by cutting costs or increasing benefits.

I emphasize *judgment* in the quest for efficiency because in higher education many of the variables, especially on the benefit side, are not quantifiable—at least not yet. Higher education is more like an art form than a profit-making enterprise. Managerial techniques that are applicable only to one side of the efficiency ratio—that is, the cost side—are of little help. What administrators in higher education desperately need is more and better knowledge of the outcomes of their efforts. They need this far more than they need modern management techniques borrowed from business. They need to know much more, both about the effects on the learning and personal development of students and about differences in the output and quality of research and public service associated with different ways of conducting higher education. In this way, their judgment could be reinforced by knowledge. The knowledge of outcomes, however, is unlikely ever to be so complete that educational decisions could be ground out of a computer. The nature of human life and education is such that the outcomes probably can never be reduced to printouts, and judgment will still be required of administrators.

A second aspect of administration is leadership, and this is as nonquantifiable as judgment. I can best illustrate leadership by the example of John Hannah of Michigan State University, whose *Memoir* was published last year.[1] He became president of Michigan State in 1941 when it was a tiny agricultural college. His previous work had been as an extension specialist in poultry husbandry and later as secretary of the board of trustees. With exceptional leadership, he was able over a mere twenty-five years to convert Michigan State into one of the nation's largest and most distinguished universities. His *Memoir* eloquently depicts the quality known as leadership and testifies to its importance in administration.

1. East Lansing: Michigan State University Press, 1980.

Surprisingly, it happens that even in the corporate world of private business, judgment and leadership are the qualities most prized in managers. Actually, this top ranking holds in organizations of all types.

The place of the so-called modern management techniques is to assist and support judgment and leadership by providing facts in an orderly fashion and by describing the range of possibilities for the future. But these techniques are not substitutes for judgment and leadership, without which organizations drift or die.

A question that must be asked is whether higher education can recruit and retain administrators with the needed qualities of judgment and leadership, given the present conditions and prospects in our industry, given the nature of the selection and recruitment procedures, and given the prevailing rewards and incentives.

The Presidential Search, A Balancing Act
Ronald S. Stead

The search today for a college or university president (system head included) has created a process that requires careful orchestration and the balancing of several competing considerations.

As the search process has become more complex, its basic purpose, the selection of outstanding leaders of institutions of higher education, has become more important than ever before. A principal concern may be institutional survival or the qualitative improvement of higher education following its unprecedented growth since World War II. Whatever the situation, care must be given to the selection of presidents and other administrators to ensure that institutions will be led in the uncertain years ahead by people who have wisdom, educational vision, strong character, and sensitivity, and who possess the skills required to manage what are complex organizations.

The present-day "national search" is pursued even by institutions that are more local than regional in character. The wide-ranging search is characterized by advertisement in national publications, committees, elaborate records, a search staff, concerns about state and federal equal employment requirements, "airport" interviews, formal visits by final candidates to the campus, and even the occasional assignment of legal counsel to the search committee. Gone are the days when the chairman of the board, possibly after informally consulting some key board and faculty members, called a prominent church official—possibly an alumnus—and invited *him* to become the next president. That was the "search." Incidentally, my emphasis on gender is a recognition of the reality that the caller and the called surely would have been males.

Whatever advantages accrued to the relatively uncomplicated selection procedures of yesteryear, there is no turning back. The worthy goals of affirmative action and shared governance dictate a presidential selection process that is far from casual and haphazard. Nonetheless, many present-day searches are conducted in a relatively unsophisticated fashion.

Aims in the Selection Process

Today's presidential search requires skillful handling and is indeed a "balancing act" if it is to produce certain important results: (1) the selection of an outstanding president for the particular institution; (2) a college community (trustees included) that supports the president because the various constituencies were satisfied with the process that led to the appointment; (3) an external community (persons solicited for nominations, public officials, references, and others involved) that has a good (or better) image of the college because they perceived the competence with which the search was conducted; and (4) a large number of persons who feel that they, as candidates, were treated with dignity, fairness, and sensitivity.

A new president who is selected as the "watered down" result of petty bickering between trustees and faculty over narrow concerns is unlikely to be a judicious choice. A faculty (could be students, alumni, church officials, administrators, or whoever) whose concerns about the search were—or at least were perceived to be—ignored probably will not be enthusiastic about the "board's" choice. A foundation executive who has submitted a nomination but received not even an acknowledgment may well wonder about the institution's manners. Finally, a candidate whose rejection comes in a mimeographed letter starting "Dear Sir or Madam" will never be a future goodwill ambassador for that institution. The above are real examples of unfortunate, insensitive acts that can undermine the desired results of a presidential search.

Some important assertions about a presidential search can, in my opinion, help create the conditions required to balance a number of desirable, but competing factors.

1. The selection of a president is the responsibility of the governing board, which must not abrogate its authority to perform what many argue is its most important task.

2. Because the shared governance concept is operative to some degree in all institutions, the governing board must involve through appropriate means the other groups (faculty, alumni, students) that reasonably expect to participate in the presidential selection.

3. Assuming that a competent president for a given institution has been appointed, the process of his or her selection determines to a large extent the effectiveness of that person as president.

4. Overinvolvement of the various groups in the selection process may be just as damaging as their underinvolvement.

5. Several biases (yes, even prejudices on occasion) operating in the presidential selection process may jeopardize the chances of appointing an outstanding leader.

6. A well-conducted selection process is closely related to an institution's ability to retain the president for a reasonable length of time.

Analysis of the above points reveals some conflicting goals in the selection of a chief executive and thus the necessity for a balancing act on the part of the governing board and the other participants. In fact, the inclination of the various groups to put the welfare of the institution as foremost in reconciling their different values, interests, and perspectives throughout the search is a prerequisite to the successful recruitment, selection, performance, and appropriate length of service of a president. While I do not press the analogy, there is the same need for legitimate unity in this selection domain as that so desperately pursued by party leaders at the 1980 national political conventions. A college or university about to embark on a search for an outstanding leader without a reasonable degree of "togetherness" among its constituencies significantly decreases the likelihood of success in the same way that the presidential candidate of a splintered political party faces decreased odds for a victory at the polls.

A critical balance must be struck between process and outcome. A sloppy process may produce an outstanding president but one who will be crippled by the means that propelled him or her into office. Conversely, overemphasis on process can detract from the essential task—the identification of a top-notch president.

A wise governing board, then, must balance its authority and responsibility for selecting the president against the need for certain constituencies, particularly the faculty, to participate if the next president is to assume office with the desired broad base of support. Yet, however well intentioned the board, the implementation of a balance between its authority and constituent involvement can be difficult. Which groups should be involved? In what number? How should they be selected? How to balance the goal of broad participation against the need for confidentiality and reasonable efficiency? These and other issues require careful thought and sensitive handling by the board in the design of a search structure.

Pitfalls in Running the Process

Boards of trustees can commit two opposite types of errors in the exercise of their authority to select a president. They may jealously and defensively guard their authority, thus keeping the faculty and others on the sidelines. Or the board may in effect delegate the task to internal groups, even omitting firm guidelines. The first type of error may be manifested along a range of actions—from outright exclusion to more subtle messages that faculty input is not likely to be taken seriously. At the other extreme, the problem may be that board members believe they do not have the required time; or perhaps a board is attempting to placate a faculty that is flexing its muscles. In either case, both the institution and the incoming president are likely to have rough sailing.

More frequent than these extreme positions are board aberrations along the way involving both types of errors. For example, the board may agree to significant faculty involvement only under pressure, which is a message to the faculty that the invitation was reluctantly issued; or some of these busy board members may miss more committee meetings than is desirable for productive results.

Many boards are reasonably successful in implementing the concept of shared governance in the presidential search process. In one institution with which I am familiar, a faculty member who was elected to serve on the joint search committee also was president of the collective bargaining unit. The institution had been in a state of serious conflict, marked by tense and acrimonious relationships. However, the presence of the union head was accepted by board members, and, to the credit of all concerned, the arrangement appeared to have been fortunate.

I have emphasized the necessity for a board to weigh its authority against the worthy concept of shared governance in the search process. Let me now "balance" that emphasis against the needs for reasonable efficiency and confidentiality in the search process.

There is a breaking point where too many participants can seriously compromise these diverse needs. At a very practical level, the larger the search committee, the more difficult it is, for example, to schedule meetings, to ensure full participation in the limited meeting time available, and to review candidate credentials.

Biases and Balances

I asserted that biases may undermine wise choices in screening candidates. What does this matter have to do with my "balancing" theme? An example may help. The search committee of College X, a public institution, rejects the candidacy of Candidate B in a perfunctory manner because B has never functioned in a public institution, the assumption being that B "can't possibly understand us." Without wishing to suggest that B's lack of experience in the public sector should not be taken into account, I believe that it is a grave mistake to judge a candidate's qualifications for a presidency on such a superficial basis. Many successful college presidents have crossed over from the public to the private sector and vice versa. After all, B may have a relatively good understanding of public higher education, personal relationships with colleagues in public institutions, and so on. Further, B may be an enlightened person who values diversity in higher education and who can be equally supportive of the public and private sectors. Further, B may have exceptional strengths pertinent to the most important selection criteria adopted by our mythical College X.

Another strong bias that normally exists, particularly among faculty members, is the high priority given to the appointment of a president who has a distinguished record of research and teaching. Yet, the personality factors, knowledge, and skills that determine presidential success may be quite unrelated to those associated with being a successful teacher-scholar. The committee should not necessarily be skeptical about candidates with strong academic records. If a candidate has all the qualifications sought by an institution, including impressive academic credentials, the composite may be a plus factor. However, the qualities of educational vision, the possession of an educational philosophy, a commitment to academic freedom, an understanding of the faculty mind, a commitment to the purposes of the particular college, and personal intelligence are the crucial traits to be sought. Distinguished scholars do not have a franchise on these qualities. In fact, it is possible that someone without a Ph.D. may possess these qualities in high measure—

eminent exceptions are proof. The point is to balance the justifiable concern about scholarly credentials against the real understanding and competences likely to be associated with presidential success *in that institution*.

Another delicate balance is to weigh the needs of the candidate against the needs of the institution. This matter has several dimensions. An inside candidate may have performed loyally and effectively at the institution and expects to have the "inside track" for the job. Yet circumstances may suggest that it would be advantageous to bring someone in from the outside who has a fresh perspective. Such a situation must be handled with considerable skill and sensitivity, for here is a person whose morale is important to his or her future relationship with the institution.

Often in a search, the candidate has a legitimate need to limit who shall know about his or her interest in the position. The institution must respect this need, but the search committee also must learn as much as possible—as soon as possible—about the candidate. There are no easy answers to this problem, and a number of variables must be taken into account. At public institutions in states with sunshine laws, the options for both parties are limited. The one fundamental principle that must be observed is for the searching institution to inform the candidate about the operational definition of confidentiality in that situation. Occasionally, a committee will have to discontinue considering a final candidate because the person has refused to permit conversations with people on his or her campus.

Several other biases or stereotypes affect the decisions of persons in the selection process. One occasionally hears the concern that a woman may not be "tough enough" to handle a particular institution; someone with a doctorate in education may be perceived as an intellectual lightweight; the candidate's degrees may be from undistinguished institutions; the person may be considered too old or too young; or the candidate's current title may not be impressive.

Over the Long Run

More biases can be added to the list. Some are fairly common; some are unique to a particular institution. To be sure, it is not a totally irrational or irresponsible inclination to favor candidates who would appear to present lower risks. Also, some fairly arbitrary decisions are required to winnow a pool of two hundred candidates, a large number of whom are well credentialed, down to a small enough group to make an in-depth analysis of their qualifications.

A frequent criticism of the balancing that runs through the current complex search task is that the surviving candidate may represent the lowest common denominator. Arguably, by the time each group eliminates persons whose qualities are least valued, including those whose strong leadership qualities may have "made waves," the survivor is distinguished only by his or her low profile of traits and achievements. The argument resembles the claim that more effective political leaders emerged in the good old days when the selecting occurred in smoke-filled rooms.

While the "worst case" allegations against today's more open, participatory search process may contain some truth, the proper response is to refine the current system rather than retreat to the former habits of selection. Thus, colleges and universities must continue to evaluate current search practices. The next balancing act is to determine whether there can be a better blend between the best features of past and present-day methods of selection. Of course, the fundamental goal, the selection of outstanding presidents, must be at the center of all efforts to improve the process.

Selecting a President—Paths and Potholes
Ruth G. Weintraub

Finding the ideal presidential candidate is the dream of every search committee. The trustees would like to find a strong budget-balancer with a charismatic personality. The faculty members seek a forward-looking educational leader who appreciates the faculty, who will make changes but not in their department or division, and who certainly will not trifle with tenure or promotional arrangements. The students would like someone who will listen to what any student has to say (without a prior appointment) and who will raise tuition only as a last resort and after major and exhaustive consultation.

Recently, additional complications and pressures have emerged that make the search process for presidents and other senior administrators particularly difficult.

Spouses and Search Committees
Jean Kemeny, in her perceptive memoir *It's Different at Dartmouth*, points out that the president's wife who entertains and

travels with her husband virtually full time for the college may be becoming an extinct phenomenon.[1] Until recently, when an institution recruited a president, it in effect recruited two people for the price of one. The wife's services were expected gratis. By 1980, we at the Academy for Educational Development found in our presidential searches that the candidate's wife can no longer be taken for granted.

The *New York Times* reported that the U.S. Department of State is having similar problems with wives of foreign service officers. The story cited several instances in which, during a tour of home duty, the officer's wife had found a job, developed a Washington real estate business, or entered law school. She jolly well did not want to go to Rabat when her husband was assigned there, so she said goodbye.[2] The State Department is still shaken.

In about three instances in 1980, we at AED encountered the same problem. One very good candidate had indicated only a week before that he could move, and when he was called on Friday, he happily iterated that he was interested in being seriously considered for an institution in Boston. He called on Monday much chagrined; his wife had said flatly that she would not leave Washington. She reminded him that she gave up her career as a fledgling singer when they were first married. She had now, a second time around, found a teacher who suited her and had clearly said that it was her turn. He did think her claim had some merit and so is staying on in a less than ideal situtation.

As another candidate put it: "My wife was an ideal wife for the 1950s. She did everything I wanted her to do, and now she is an appropriate wife for the 1970s. She does exactly what she wants to do." He added that she has a great job in Washington and would want to weigh whether the job for which he was being considered would have so many pluses for him that she would be willing to give up her job and chance finding a new one. Under such a standard, no job seemed good enough for him.

In a third case, a combination of the wife's excellent job and their beautiful house in a Boston suburb appeared to make the candidate ambivalent. When he talked to the trustees of a New York institution, they could not decide whether he really wanted the job. He did.

1. Brattleboro, Vt.: Stephen Greene Press, 1979.

2. Leslie Bennetts, "Foreign Service Wives: Many Are Choosing to Remain Behind," May 11, 1979.

Now that women are being appointed to presidencies, helping the husband find a suitable professorship or other position becomes a delicate task for the search committee. Search committees have learned the hard way that a departmental appointments committee will dig in their collective heels if even a suggestion is made that the president's spouse, male or female, is a suitable candidate for the department.

Is it appropriately a concern of a search committee if the candidate is a woman and her husband cannot or will not relocate? What will happen to their marriage? Or if the situation is reversed and the candidate is a man and the wife has a career in a city several hundred miles away? These may be troublesome questions for search committees.

Presidential Housing

Has the housing become too costly? Or how is the housing situation handled when the last president set up too extravagant a life style? Some search committees are faced with the practical problem that the last president had set up an opulent life style that contrasted too sharply with faculty housing and salaries. Should the mansion be sold and a more modest home purchased for the new president? Such realistic questions should be settled before candidates are interviewed.

Some search committees have found ex-presidents have become so attached to the institution that they do not want to leave the campus. When sentimental trustees make arrangements (often secret) with outgoing presidents, they then present the incoming president with awkward situations that make it difficult for him or her to stay and remain satisfied with the position.

Educational Costs

Educational benefits for the president's children and other perquisites help make a presidential salary package a work of art and one of mystery. Institutions are very secretive about presidential "perks." Although administrative compensation surveys have helped unveil presidential salaries, the extras are guarded secrets. Clubs, gardeners, tuition for wives and children, expense accounts, travel, insurance, deferred compensation plans—all are part of what, in the independent sector at least, continue to be closely guarded secrets.

Guidelines for Search Committees

The suggestions that follow are based on eight years of professional experience in helping some sixty institutions search for chief executive officers, preceded by twelve years as a liberal arts dean, during which time recruitment was a major component of my position. Drawing on that background, I can say that search committees are advised to decide, before candidates are interviewed, how to address the spouse, housing, and other cost problems. In addition, the following should serve as guides for conduct.

• Search committees tend to spend too much time and energy in developing a blueprint of an ideal candidate and thus slow down the entire search process. Their energies exhausted by the exercise, they tend never to look at the document again but become entranced by the first charismatic personality.

• Some institutions set up too complicated a structure for search purposes. Institutions are well advised to avoid having two or three separate committees for different constituencies. In my experience, one search committee with representation from trustees, faculty, alumni, and students works much more smoothly and with greater harmony. From the outset, it must be made clear that the search committee's role is advisory only.

• Search committees should avoid zeroing in on one candidate. They should at all times be considering at least three qualified candidates. The reason is obvious. The only candidate may suddenly evaporate and thus leave the committee desperate and too willing to accept the next available candidate.

• Search committees should not underestimate the need for independent and intensive investigation of candidates, nor should they be tempted to make nominations because the search is taking longer than anticipated. Rather than make an appointment that the institution will regret, the wiser course is to appoint an acting president.

• Trustees on the search committee who are ready to make an offer to a presidential candidate should be absolutely frank about the financial conditions at the institution and any other facts of life (for example, financial arrangements to encourage the prior president to resign, and the like). Nothing is more frustrating to a new incumbent than to find out about these situations after accepting the position.

• The trustees who have authority to make an offer of a position should discuss frankly with the candidate what is expected and in how many years. The candidate should be told how he will be evaluated and by whom. With these matters clear, the institution has a chance for a happy relationship.

Continuity in Executive Staffing in Higher Education
Jacqueline Grennan Wexler

Planning for executive staffing and continuity in that staffing has been almost taboo in the academic world. Even when we in the higher education community began to take other aspects of long-range planning seriously, we failed to make succession in leadership part of that planning process.

That failure is clearly evident in an otherwise excellent planning document on higher education submitted in 1980 to the general assembly of a northeastern state. Entitled *Anticipating the 1980's*, the review, analysis, and recommendations cover the case for change; a new proposal for the governance of state colleges and universities; and policy positions and proposals on program, facilities, and fiscal planning, and on equity and access. In the section dealing with economic issues, the report does draw attention to the personnel-intensive nature of all colleges and universities. "On the average," the report states, "83 percent of each constituent unit operating budget is dedicated to personal services," and it points up the limited flexibility to shift resources that results from this concentration of budget on personnel.

Yet nowhere does the document address the quality of executive management needed to lead these personnel-intensive institutions. The example is fairly typical of the failure of long-range planning efforts in higher education to recognize executive leadership as a major consideration.

Incredible as the omission would appear to sophisticated observers, it is not surprising to most professionals who have lived their lives inside the academic world. When executive leadership has been strong, sensitive, and supportive of its most creative faculty, that leadership has been quietly taken for granted in good times and held rigorously responsible in bad times. In that respect, the role of leaders is extraordinarily similiar in corporations, government, and colleges and universities. One positive consequence of bad times is a renewed recognition of the need for leadership and the importance of keeping leadership and management coupled in the same person.

Corporation Planning for Leadership

Planning for executive leadership has long been regarded by business corporations as the very lifeline of healthy institutions. When the nature of the corporation is personnel-intensive, when creativity and imagination are at the heart of the enterprise, the need for strong, sensitive, supportive leadership is especially acute. Boards of directors and their compensation committees spend considerable time and intense effort in working with the chief executive officers to be sure that procedures for finding, nurturing, and sustaining those leaders are in place and in practice.

In healthy corporations, both corporate and divisional executives, in setting performance standards for themselves and for those who report to them, give high priority to planning for succession in their ranks. In the annual review of performance objectives, an important evaluative criterion is the relative readiness of one or two back-up people to step into the executive's position, should he or she be promoted or move elsewhere.

When the corporation includes distinct divisions or integrated companies, the chief executive is acutely aware that the divisional leaders must understand the common and the distinctive qualities of the units both in their competition with each other and in their interdependence on one another. No amount of dicta by a board of directors or of stockholder resolutions will compensate for the lack of this kind of corporate leadership.

Most healthy corporations, when making a broad search, do not restrict themselves to considering only the in-house candidates, but they do count on having high-quality candidates in the ranks against whom they measure outsiders.

Intellectual Leadership and Effective Management

Qualities of leadership and management are far less clearly defined in the university world. Anyone who has participated in a committee search for a university president or dean is keenly aware of the unresolved faculty tensions over executive leadership in university administration. Able faculty members rightly insist on an intellectual leader, a person capable of communicating with them and for them on the ferment of ideas that is the very heart of a university. Because faculty members, with few exceptions, have come to intellectual maturity through academic research (first in the pursuit of their Ph.D's and sustained in their professional lives), they believe that their leaders most often will have traveled similar paths. Faculties are beginning to recognize, however, that universities are large, complex organizations that must be well managed, well supported, and well interpreted to multiple constituencies if they are to survive and prosper under the intense competition for available resources.

Where does one find these intellectual leaders who are or can be good managers, good fund raisers, good representatives of the enterprise? Most college and university presidents today came to their posts from a presidency elsewhere or from a deanship in their own or another institution. Hanna Gray was provost at Yale before becoming president at Chicago. Donald Kennedy rose from provost to the presidency at Stanford, and Michael Sovern followed the same route at Columbia. Occasionally, an elegant professor is plucked from the faculty ranks of his or her institution when the board and the faculty representatives are convinced that perceived talent will make up for the lack of a track record in administration. Bartlett Giamatti at Yale was such a choice.

Long after the president has assumed office, the search committee and the responsible board will know how effectively they have reconciled the tensions between intellectual leadership and effective management in their choice among candidates. They will never know how much the widespread confusion and lack of clarity about the importance of these talents stunted the growth and development of the candidates they considered. Unless all of us in higher education—trustees, faculties, administrators, and private and public support groups—begin to make concern for the quality executive leadership central to our planning process in the future, we will continue to pay a high price for doing the best we can with the available talent.

Developing Criteria for Executive Leadership

In evaluating presidential careers for their effects on all higher education, I would give very high marks to those who played strong roles in developing future leaders for their own or other institutions. I suspect few did so with great deliberation, and no one in the past could attempt straightforwardly to develop successors without that action becoming the "kiss of death" for the suspected protégés. It is time we face up to the negative influence that this kind of attitude has on the development of a leadership pool for higher education.

No president of a college or a university should name—directly or indirectly—his or her own successor. Every good president should, however, work hard to develop a strong administration in whose ranks will be potential candidates for his own or similar positions. When search committees go outside to develop the richest possible pool of candidates, they should be able to measure the abilities of the outsiders against strong inside contenders.

Thoughtful faculty members interested in the long-term health of their own universities and in the health and public image of higher education as a whole would not, I believe, reject honest and professional planning for succession in executive leadership. There would always be the possibility of selecting a highly talented professor in an institution if the search committee and the board were convinced that his or her clear talent was a better bet than the more comprehensive track record of proven executives in the intellectual community. To make that bet prudently, however, the deliberative bodies should have been able to measure the atypical candidates by some clear norms of performance. The judgment could be made with more assuredness had the talent been recognized earlier and the potential candidate been placed in a situation in which to grow and perform.

The corollary of that proposition is equally valid. If a candidate with an impressive record in executive leadership outside the walls of academe is to be seriously considered, the deliberative bodies should be able to judge the potential strength of the candidate as an intellectual leader. Trustees and faculty members can and must determine some clear norms for judging the ability of such a candidate to communicate with the faculty in the world of ideas.

The academic enterprise must not be forced to make a choice between an intellectual leader or an effective manager to lead the nation's colleges and universities. *Either/or* is not good enough. Only *both/and* can succeed. The depth of proven ability on each scale will vary from candidate to candidate and should vary from position to position. There are no 10s in executive leadership. Unlike beauty contests or gymnastic performances, the criteria for judgment are too complex to pretend that perfect performers exist. We can, however, begin to describe substantively what we are looking for and to judge candidates by their proven records and perceived talent to meet these substantive qualities. Academic credentials and administrative records will lead us to many (but not all) of the worthwhile candidates. In my opinion, the number of able candidates inside the traditional pool would be greatly increased in the future if we defined academic leadership with the same intellectual rigor we demand in other academic pursuits and if we approached the development and the selection of these leaders with the same professionalism for which we take pride in all other areas of the university world. Even more important, the staying and growing power of presidents during their terms of office would be greatly enhanced.

Toward Definition

If faculties, in word or in practice, disdain the importance of management in their defense of the intellectual life, the intellectual life will be mismanaged by the inability of academic leaders to cope with the complex constituencies on whom their institutions depend. If legislatures and educational bureaucracies demand managers who are incapable of sharing in the intellectual life of their institutions, that life will be squandered for lack of sensitive and creative nurturing.

There are young men and women capable of becoming executive statesmen. We will find them, test them, and choose them provided we set long-range goals for academic leadership worthy of their talents and supportive of their development.

I lead a consulting and search firm focused on higher education but shall not here discuss the mechanics of the search process. We there are convinced that the quality of a presidential search depends on the clear development of institutional leadership strategies by the trustees and faculty. We urge institutions, if possible, to address this undertaking long before a president resigns or retires. Experienced professional consultants can focus the planning effort, which should:
- *Define* and understand institutional objectives, both present and future;
- *Clarify* and refine the administrative structure of the institution;
- *Assure* that job specifications are prepared and that performance standards are established for each key administrative position;
- *Review* compensation and benefit levels for these positions; and,
- *Develop* procedures for search and selection when vacancies occur.

If those leadership strategies are not in place when the presidency opens, we urge institutions to develop them before the search is formally launched. Once the issues are clear and precise, a rich candidate pool appropriate to the specific challenges and opportunities of the institution can be identified. Experienced consultants provide professional support in identifying candidates and in maintaining the confidentiality without which many of the most highly qualified candidates will be lost.

Search that recognizes the collegial nature of colleges and universities and develops a professionalism appropriate to collegial structure will identify and recruit candidates who can lead and manage those institutions. The process of developing institutional strategies for executive staffing will do much to clarify the role, the expectancies, and the demands of the presidency. Nothing will do more to keep a president productive than a clear consensus about the nature and functioning of the role he or she assumes.

Identifying Talented Women
Carolyn L. Ellner

The past decade has seen the passage of equal employment legislation and affirmative action regulations that increase the opportunities of women to swim in the talent pool from which academic administrators are chosen. Since presidential years in office at colleges and universities are declining, the next decade should be a time of opportunity for talented women to assume leadership roles in postsecondary education.

The annual turnover rate for presidents is approximately 14 percent, and the rate for systemwide presidencies is a little higher at 17 percent.[1] Only 16 percent of those who leave go on to another presidency.[2] Theoretically, by the end of the 1980s the hope might be to fill close to 50 percent of high academic administrative vacancies with women, that is, of course, if women still hold the belief that such positions were fulfilling, effective, and rewarding.

I wish to acknowledge the assistance of Diana Lockard, who helped clarify many ideas in this paper through lively discussion and debate.

1. Joseph F. Kauffman, *At the Pleasure of the Board* (Washington: American Council on Education, 1980), p. 16.

2. *Chronicle of Higher Education*, September 29, 1980, p. 6.

At present, women represent about 25 percent of the professoriat.[3] Even with this substantial, albeit modest pool, only 214, or 7 percent, of approximately 3,000 colleges and universities are headed by women.[4] However, since 1975 the number of women presidents has increased by 28 percent, with the greatest leap forward in the public sector, where the increase has been about 200 percent. In numbers, in 1975 five women were presidents of four-year public colleges and now there are fourteen; eleven women were presidents of two-year public colleges, and now there are thirty-three.[5]

Women have come a long way since Congresswoman Edith Green held the first hearing on sex discrimination in 1970. At that time not one member of the education establishment came forward to testify—because sex discrimination on campus was not a problem.[6] We have, of course, not come far enough.

If the gene pool is equally distributed and women as well as men possess the technical and interpersonal skills necessary for effective leadership (a finding substantiated by Kanter[7]), we must conclude that talent alone will be insufficient to close the gap between men and women in academic administration. While talent is essential, it must be *recognized* by those who make the decisions about who will lead educational institutions.

I have reviewed the literature on administrative searches and reflected on my own experience. I have participated in many searches, several of them academic, but some of them administrative. From older reports such as *How College Presidents Are Chosen*, I realize how far the search process has evolved over the last few decades. In that book, Frederick deW. Bolman describes the search process as it was carried out in 1960 in over a hundred and fifteen colleges and universities. His view of the talent pool and his determination to find "the right man" would raise anxiety in any enlight-

3. Judith M. Gappa and Barbara S. Uehling, *Women in Academe: Steps to Greater Equality*, AAHE-ERIC/Higher Education Research Report, no. 1, 1979 (Washington: American Association for Higher Education, 1979), p. 43.

4. Emily Taylor, Donna Shavlik, and Judith Touchton, "S-L-O-W but Steady," *Comment*, June 1980, p. 9.

5. Ibid.

6. George W. Bonham et al., eds., *Women on Campus: The Unfinished Liberation* (New Rochelle, N.Y.: Change Magazine Press, 1975), p. 9.

7. R. M. Kanter, *Men and Women of the Corporation* (New York: Basic Books, 1977), p. 9.

ened searcher today. The need for the candidate to have "a good wife" would also cause discomfort.[8]

Bringing women into consideration as strong and viable candidates will, I believe, not take place without deliberate strategies designed to confer legitimacy and respect on the candidates. There are several points in the search process where enlightened candidates and equally enlightened searchers might be more effective in increasing the visibility and viability of candidates. Competent women exist. Their talents must be examined in an unbiased, undistorted light.

Getting Women on the List

The first challenge for a candidate is to be placed in consideration. *Chronicle of Higher Education* and *New York Times Supplement on Education*, among others, play a large part in announcing searches and inviting application. They serve a useful, necessary purpose but are insufficient. Other mechanisms, nondiscriminating in character, are needed to distinguish promising candidates from others. Identification made by someone who can match institutional needs with individual talent is a valuable asset to a search committee. Although the "old boy network" has been criticized as being exclusionary, still it serves a useful purpose. It should be kept alive and thriving, but its perspective broadened. Until women are in positions of power in large numbers, they will have to persuade men in power that there are competent and talented women to whom these men should be committed. For example, Chancellor Gary Hays of the Minnesota State System has, in his years of office, advanced many women to positions of influence in higher education. One of them, a Claremont Graduate School alumna, is now president of Mankato State University.

The National Identification Program created by the Office of Women in Higher Education of the American Council on Education has succeeded in making women more visible for consideration for administrative positions.[9] Through a system of personal identification and recognition, the program has been committed to advancing women into policy-making positions. Its influence has been and will be forcefully felt in our colleges and universities. The program was

8. Washington: American Council on Education, 1967.

9. Judith Touchton and Donna Shavlik, "Challenging the Assumptions of Leadership: Women and Men of the Academy," *New Directions for Higher Education*, no. 22 (1978), pp. 95–106.

initiated in 1977 in twelve states and now encompasses forty-seven states, Puerto Rico, New York City, and Washington, D.C. At the National Forums—a part of the program—talented women have made significant contacts with influential persons in policy and governance in education, as well as made friendships and contacts that have helped to promote career opportunities.

Other networks are evolving. Three HERS (Higher Education Resource Services) groups now exist—one in New England, one in the Mid-Atlantic region, and one, the most recent, in the West. There are, as well, concerns groups in New England, New York, and California. They differ in membership, organizational structure, and activities but are united in a commitment to the advancement of women in higher education administration. All offer opportunities for women to learn about job openings, to come together for moral support, and to enhance their management skills.

Women are often at a disadvantage because of the nature and form of the criteria, both explicit and implicit, against which a person is to be measured. The literature notes many qualities sought in selecting top administrators. Among them are scholarly competence, fund-raising ability, expertise in financial management, and skill in academic planning, human relations, and personnel management. That is quite a list for a job that Nobel Laureate Herbert Simon has described as one for an "amateur." According to Simon, "Comparing colleges with other organizations in our society, one sees that their most striking peculiarity is not their product, but the extent to which they are run by amateurs. They are institutions run by amateurs to train professionals."[10]

Certainly, candidates should be evaluated for the above-mentioned administrative competences, rather than on traditional experience and training, such as "previous dean's-level experience." In this regard, the trend toward criteria dealing with operations is helpful.

Besides explicit criteria are implicit criteria, those derived from our cultural biases, to which even the most committed feminist may be subject. On an emotional level, women may, as a result of early acculturation, tend to agree with such statements as, "It is easier to work for a man" or "The top administrator of an organization should create an authoritative, aggressive, and wise image." These assump-

10.   Herbert Simon, "The Job of a College President," *Educational Record*, Winter 1967, p. 69.

tions are, however, not borne out in practice; in fact, it is the organization's members who tend to imbue their leaders with such qualities.

One further comment about criteria. If few women apply for a position, in my view, it is incumbent on the search committee to review its formal criteria for biases against women.

A Context for Evaluating Women Candidates

The judgment of vitae is another area where talented women may be at a disadvantage. Because a woman may have assumed many roles in her early adult years, a vita may look disjointed. A woman is more likely to begin a career in one direction, take time out for a family, and start off in another direction late. When such a vita is compared with a more traditional one, it may look weak; in truth, it may demonstrate desirable traits such as flexibility and a tolerance for ambiguity.

Vita appraisal should also consider whether "more is better." Research has shown that women are more likely than men to be at teaching institutions rather than at research universities. Where the primary emphasis is on teaching, publications usually assume lesser importance. Is quantity as important as quality? How many articles are "enough" to show that one is a competent scholar?

A search committee relies heavily on the source of a candidate's nomination and on references. The greatest attention goes to communications from distinguished persons, well known in the academic world, or to high-level administrators who may be less widely known, but whose judgment is trusted because they are personally known. Unfortunately, it is easier for a man to know such persons of influence because usually they, too, are men. The ACE's National Identification Program, noted above, is making it easier for women to meet in task-oriented groups with the movers and shakers in education.

Another critical point in the search process is the interview. At this point the implicit criteria and personal prejudices may make a difference. Feminine characteristics are interpreted differently from masculine ones: He is firm, she is stubborn; he is adaptive, she is vacillating; he is forceful, she is abrasive; he is congenial, she is cloying.

A woman's physical stature may influence decisions based on face-to-face contact. A tall woman may seem threatening, and a small woman weak. A well-dressed woman may appear to place too much emphasis on unessential matters, and a poorly dressed woman may be described as a slattern.

Getting to the short list of candidates is indeed an honor. Paradoxically, a woman may be included in the group, not for merit, but solely to satisfy affirmative action requirements. Such action does no favor to the woman or to the advancement of women; rather, the reverse. Since I firmly believe there are competent women in the pool, if a less than well-qualified woman makes the short list, something may have been quite wrong at an earlier point in the search process. If votes for the short list are secret (they often are), the selection or rejection of a woman becomes a matter of conscience. The final selection depends on the wisdom of the board members, their sensitivity, and their ability to separate what is relevant from what is not. Without commitment to the advancement of the best persons, institutions will not utilize all those with talent. As a consequence, they will be limiting the potential future of post-secondary education.

A word about talent and women. A powerful point was made by Robert Schrank of the Ford Foundation in "Two Women, Three Men on a Raft." In the first six pages of his article, one wonders what an Outward Bound trip down the Rogue River had to do with administrative talent and women's leadership. All persons on the raft were supposed to share tasks equally, including rowing, gathering wood, cooking, and serving as helmsperson. Under the guise of increasing efficiency and promoting the good of the group, the men subtly and unconsciously, with all the good will in the world, undermined the women's opportunity to do "men's work," such as guiding the raft.[11]

The insight gained concerned the level of peer and subordinate support. Weaknesses in the men were compensated for by helping them improve their skills; weaknesses in the women were met with attempts to take over their responsibility and thereby compensate for their inefficiency.

> It became clear to me that not only had I been unhappy with a woman as helmsperson, but also that Bill and I had subconsciously, by habit, proceeded to undermine the women. When one of the other two men was in charge, I was comfortable, supportive, and worked to help him be a better helmsperson. When a woman was at the helm, I seemed to direct my activity at getting her replaced rapidly by one of the men. [p. 107]

11. *Harvard Business Review*, May-June 1977, pp. 100–8.

Particularly with regard to subordinates, Schrank makes the point that it is possible to cooperate at different levels—to create a facade of cooperation to mask a lack of support, a dangerous deception. A female administrator makes a tough decision based on her best judgment, but unless she has full support by subordinates, her decision is sabotaged and in the end might as well never have been made. The lesson is clear, though how to cope with the problem is less so. Schrank suggests that the place to start is by working to raise and change the consciousness of men of good will who hold power and who, without recognizing their unconscious biases, are unlikely to allow women to join the competition for advancement on an equal basis.

Many talented women as well as men are eager to contribute to the advancement of higher education. Our past cultural biases may have narrowed our perspective. It is now time to be open to new ideas and new opportunities to choose our leaders from an enriched supply.

FACULTY UNIONS

The Ambiguities of Winning and Losing—
Yeshiva
Blanche D. Blank

On February 20, 1980, the United States Supreme Court arrived at a decision that the media instantly pronounced seminal. In *NLRB* v. *Yeshiva University*,[1] the Court, by a five to four majority, decided that the faculty of Yeshiva University was management and therefore not able to unionize under the terms of the National Labor Relations Act (NLRA). There is, however, both more and less here than is suggested at first glance.

First and foremost, the basic problems that gave rise to the case are unsolved by the decision. Second, there are very significant boundaries to the scope of the decision itself. Third, some legal issues remain obscure. Finally, certain administrative and operational procedures may be made more complex by the uncertainties as well as by the conclusions of the decision.

The point to bear in mind in this connection is that all of us in higher education must wrestle directly with the root problem of a growing disparity between individual and institutional definitions of purposeful and healthful university survival. If we fail to diminish the energy-sapping internal battles that are being waged on all too many campuses (unionized as well as nonunionized, of which this case is an example), we shall be unable to address the real war—the war for society's continued and improved understanding and support. Without that broad support, education as a whole, and higher education in particular, is threatened. Internecine warfare reduces our credibility and contributes to public criticism.

I shall return later to the underlying problems. Let me deal first with the demographic backdrop to the decision before discussing its meaning in legal terms.

At present approximately six hundred institutions of higher education are unionized. Most are two-year colleges; more are in the

1. Natl. Labor Relations Board v. Yeshiva University, 444 U.S. 672 (1980).

public sector than in the private. Indeed, only seventy-seven private colleges and universities are unionized. Viewed another way, out of 665,000 faculty members, 130,000 are in unions.[2] The largest union is the American Federation of Teachers, which is the bargaining agent for such "biggies" as City University of New York, State University of New York, the Florida university system, and the Pennsylvania state colleges. Other unions are the American Association of University Professors and the National Education Association.

Although the legislation involved in the Yeshiva University case is the National Labor Relations Act, passed in 1935, twenty-four states have legislation covering their public sector colleges. The NLRA does not directly specify universities; higher education has been read in, so to speak, by the National Labor Relations Board and certain court decisions over the past nine years.

The Decision

What precisely did the Supreme Court say? It said that the faculty at a particular university, namely Yeshiva, was management and therefore its members were not entitled to unionize under the protection of the National Labor Relations Board. The majority of the Court, led by Justice Lewis Powell, were not persuaded by the NLRB's argument that the faculty was not managerial because its members acted only in *group* decision-making contexts, and that they acted out of their own self-interest, not the university's. In the course of their opinion, the majority had things to say about "mature" universities (presumably those that hewed more closely to an image of the medieval model) and distinguished the full-time tenured faculty from the untenured and part-time. All these factors hedge the decision. Significantly, too, the decision refers only to institutions in the private sector.

As viewed by Justice Powell and his associates:

The controlling consideration in this case is that the faculty of Yeshiva University exercise authority which in any other context unquestionably would be managerial. This authority in academic matters is absolute. They decide what courses will be offered, when they will be scheduled, and to whom they will be taught. They debate and determine teaching methods, grading policies, and matriculation standards. They effectively decide which students will be admitted, retained, and graduated. On occasion their views

2. Gene I. Maeroff, "Taking Stock After *Yeshiva*," *Educational Record*, Summer 1980, p. 16.

have determined the size of the student body, the tuition to be charged, and the location of a school.

The minority, led by Justice Brennan, seemed more attuned to today's realities when they astutely remarked that

Whatever influence the faculty wields in university decision making is attributable solely to their collective expertise as professional educators, and not to any managerial or supervisory prerogatives. . . . the faculty offers its recommendations in order to serve its own independent interest in creating the most effective environment for learning, teaching, and scholarship. And while the administration may attempt to defer to the faculty's competence whenever possible, it must and does apply its own distinct perspective to those recommendations, a perspective that is based on fiscal and other managerial policies which the faculty has no part in developing.

The minority understood the essential truth that

Unlike industrial supervisors and managers, university professors are not hired to make operative the policies and decisions of their employer. . . . Faculty members are judged by their employer on the quality of their teaching and scholarship, not on the compatability of their advice with administration policy. . . . Education has become "big business," and the task of operating the university has been transferred from the faculty to an autonomous administration which faces the same pressures to cut costs and increase efficiencies that confront any large industrial organization. . . . Economic exigencies have also exacerbated the tensions in university labor relations as the faculty and administration more and more frequently find themselves advocating conflicting positions not only on issues of compensation, job security, and working conditions, but even on subjects formerly thought to be the faculty's prerogative.

The financial facts of life at Yeshiva University were also better assessed by the minority in citing some comparative salary figures that helped to clarify the perspective in which the case had arisen. Thus, while I do not agree with that portion of the minority opinion that refers to an "autonomous administration" (I do not believe such a thing exists), I essentially do subscribe to their view of academic reality rather than the model imagined by the majority. (I must say I would indeed prefer life at a campus sufficiently "mature" to preclude the need for unions.)

The paradoxical kernel in the case has been well stated by one of Yeshiva's own faculty members, Paul Connolly, associate professor of English. He has often explained that the Yeshiva faculty had to insist that they were nonmanagerial and nonsupervisory in order to

organize themselves into a body that could reassert its managerial
and supervisory power. He adds further, it has been the administration, paradoxically, that insisted that the faculty *is* managerial and
supervisory in order to restrict faculty power.

In short, if the faculty were to be declared rank and file
employees, they would apparently be able to make a successful bid to
exert managerial functions. It would thus appear that a union's very
success would also be its demise.

Possible Ripple Effects and Procedural Complexities

From the time the action commenced to the time the decision
was issued took about seven years. It will take longer for the decision
to be clarified, but in the next decade, the effects will become
manifest. And those effects will impinge on politicians, professors,
unions, administrators, other professionals, and ultimately students
and the public. First of all, the developments will give rise to new
legislative activity. By early fall 1980, a bill had already been
proposed in the House of Representatives to amend the NLRA
specifically to include colleges and universities. If the act is so
modified, the decision would, in effect, be nullified. What is more
likely to happen—and to happen in the next few years—is legislative
activity on the state level. In the twenty-six states that have not
spoken on the issue, the decision may have a paralyzing effect. States
with laws protecting unionization in their public universities will
probably see increased lobbying to maintain or strengthen such acts
and possibly broaden their scope.

Some analysts feel that the *Yeshiva* decision foreshadows similar
restraints in other areas; thus, health care facilities, orchestras,
engineering establishments, and social work agencies may soon find
that their main personnel are also managerial and thus not the stuff
of which unions are made.

More immediate effects are evident on campuses around the
nation. In fall 1980, University of Albuquerque was told by the
NLRB that its faculty members were indeed managerial and therefore the board's services would be unavailable. Villanova withdrew
from its forthcoming NLRB bargaining. Adrian College in Michigan, New Haven College in Connecticut, Ithaca College in New
York, and Boston University each backed off from collective bargaining negotiations. Indeed, more than thirty cases pending before
the NLRB have been or will be affected.

The decision may have effects on the unions. Perhaps in the face of this kind of threat, they will merge, as did the AFL and CIO following passage of the Taft-Hartley Act. On the other hand, perhaps, the AAUP will feel it has a special advantage to go it alone because of its long history as a prestigious professional guild that predates its union pretensions.

But most important are the possible effects the case will have in the immediate future on typical day-to-day academic processes faced by faculties and administrations. On the one hand, the faculty, by apparently losing the case, may actually win its basic demands. While all faculty struggles include a strong economic component, an equally strong component (or so most faculties, including Yeshiva's, claim) concerns decision making, governance, and similar issues. Thus, a university would have to produce an array of management prerogatives in order to qualify as a "mature" university under the umbrella of the Court's decision. Moreover, according to a common principle, the less that is prescribed, the more the power implied. A long, explicit union contract may offer less freedom of action than a set of tacitly accepted conventions. In these ways faculties may have won greater power.

On the other hand, it is equally possible (and more convention-ally expected) that management's hand will be strengthened, per-haps principally because the case underlined certain elements of faculty-management arrangements. For one thing, the decision notes that top management is under still higher authority—the trustees. Such understanding strengthens the administration when-ever faculty opinions are overturned. Further, inasmuch as the majority opinion hung entirely on the faculty as managerial rather than supervisory, the implication might be that a faculty could be denied supervisory prerogatives and still participate in the medieval model that enjoins unionization. Note here that the Court's majority explicitly pointed out they were *not* dealing with the question of supervisory powers, and they footnoted as qualification that supervi-sory powers include such matters as hiring, firing, and workload. This distinction may weaken faculty prerogatives. Next, in those situtations where management still elects to bargain, it now has an additional option. If things are not going well, management can threaten simply to stop bargaining. Finally, the view might emerge that a unionized faculty is by definition a faculty clearly *not* at the core of university life. In such instances the faculty can no longer claim, as did Columbia University's in admonishing President Eisenhower, "We are the university." These are the possible losses to the faculty.

The most overriding effect, however, is probably a serious and potentially negative one for all concerned. In the short run we shall probably see an increase in litigation on the one hand, and heavy pressure politics on the other. There seems to be less incentive all around to sit down and reason collectively. The decision has created as many uncertainties as clarifications. And uncertainty is usually less tolerable than unpleasantness.

Among the new questions bred by the case (in addition to those noted above):

- When does a faculty association become a union?
- What will or can happen to a group of faculty members not protected by the NLRB if they should choose to strike or take some other job action?
- What will or can happen in those places where part-time or untenured faculty members, who, under this decision, may be viewed as nonmanagerial, decide to unionize, whereas their colleagues cannot?
- Will the private-public tensions in higher education increase?
- Will the decision have indirect but important effects on the scope of bargaining in those institutions, both public and private, where unions are still extant?

Basic Problems Left Unsolved

As stated at the outset, the decision did not address several underlying issues in the case, and to my mind these issues are the key to the future. Specifically, I see in the 1980s an unfortunate confluence of two trends: Money running out; bureaucracy running in. Rising inflation reduces the real spendable income available for many services, disproportionately so for higher education. Between 1970 and 1979 philanthropic giving in the United States from all sources for *all* purposes increased from $20 billion to $43 billion—a raw growth rate of 8.5 percent, but only 1.6 percent when inflation is factored in. As a percentage of the gross national product, giving declined from 2.01 percent in 1970 to 1.83 percent in 1979.[3] Coupled with this decline is the down trend of enrollments with its attendant loss of tuition and capitation grants. Thus, the revenue shortfall.

3. E. B. Knauft, "Looking into the Eighties," *Foundation News*, July/August 1980, p. 26.

Also bureaucratization is increasing in all sectors of American life, again hitting our colleges and universities disproportionately hard. This latter trend exacerbates the eroding effects of inflation. While dollar cutbacks may cause a shock to faculty members accustomed to the expansionism of the 1960s and early 1970s, increasing bureaucracy is an even greater shock, flouting as it does many centuries of the collegial ideal. Gone are the days of either the medieval model (as envisioned by the Supreme Court brethren) or even of old-fashioned paternalism à la Nicholas Murray Butler. Enter the era of what Cohen and March call "organized anarchy," or what Bunzel describes as "industrialized democracy."[4] These latter styles, however, are based on parochialism, power, pressure politics, and organizational formalities, rather than the older tradition of collegial persuasion, founded on reason. The very processes by which universities reform themselves yield relentlessly to perversion. Every reform ironically breeds its own corruption. The endless participatory meetings of increasingly large groups of interest representatives, for example, have contributed to the ultimate powerlessness of each of these groups individually and of all of them collectively. Stalemate is thus becoming the typical outcome of many well-meant reforms.

Moreover, the reforms of our larger society have, themselves, produced the bureaucratic hierarchies within the universities about which we all complain. The need for greater public accountability and for maneuverability among frequently opposing sets of public directives has caused extraordinary administrative proliferations. Some examples: Personnel offices abound where old-fashioned department chairmen used to suffice. And hiring secretaries today is no easy matter; ads and notices must be placed publicly and internally. Care must be taken not to infringe on the procedures of nondiscrimination legislation as well as affirmative action rules, each of which often contradicts the other. For similar reasons, labor relations offices, affirmative action offices, government relations offices, and legal counsel offices have been born and enlarged in the typical fashion of Parkinson's Law. Social Security legislation, occupational safety legislation, truth-in-testing legislation, truth-in-advertising legislation, retirement legislation, health care legislation, wage and hour legislation—each in turn breeds its public bureaucracies on

4. Michael D. Cohen and James G. March, *Leadership and Ambiguity: The American College President* (New York: McGraw-Hill, 1974), pp. 2–4; John H. Bunzel, *Anti-Politics in America*, reprint ed. (Westport, Conn.: Greenwood, 1979).

national, state, and local levels, and engenders also a responsive bureaucracy inside our ivy-covered walls. When the faculty complains that administrative ranks seem to grow at a much faster pace than do faculty ranks, they are right. But the reasons are often outside the genuine control of even the university's president. These basic problems are particularly grave since they are resistant to "good guy versus bad guy" analyses. Survey evidence confirms that both presidents and professors feel equally powerless in the wake of ever larger waves of extrainstitutional intrusions.

The specific issues of the Yeshiva University case thus stemmed from two trends: reduced resources and increased bureaucracy. The faculty members' increasing sense of insecurity and their increasing sense of powerlessness were the immediate incentives for unionization. They sought to organize only after experiencing a series of what they viewed as assaults on their salaries, their job security, and their control over the key ingredients of their working conditions. The faculty did not realize that university administrators shared these feelings. Faculty alienation, however, was particularly acute. All the usual symptoms appeared: distrust of all authority, withdrawal from institutional mores, and increasing escapism.

Now, more than half a decade later, many new characters in the drama on the administrative side have appeared. The legal case has been decided. Yet the faculty is still unhappy about salary, security, and working conditions. The vice president for academic affairs (myself) must still try to negotiate with the faculty in regard to all of these issues. Had there been a union, such negotiation would, of course, have been necessary. Without one, it is equally necessary. Since so much depends on actual fiscal capacity and on faculty and administration attitudes, it is hard to believe that the presence or absence of a union would have made much difference either in the day-to-day activities of the university or on the ultimate outcomes.

The Long-Run View

The somewhat uplifting notion that "less is more" establishes difficult parameters for any negotiation. Yet that is the task besetting almost every college and university for the next three or four years. Data for the longer future are far less secure, but we can hope for an increasingly larger pie by the 1990s. Until that time, however, the insecurity of faculties and administrations will be incessant and predominant. It will be the uninvited guest at every meeting—whether among union or nonunion personnel. This essential dilemma makes the survival of universities as institutions a variable independent, so it seems, of the survival of its members. Indeed sometimes the survival of the whole appears to command the death of some of its parts.

Not only are fewer traditional students arriving on campus, but even within that shrinking cohort there are also major dislocations being caused by the students in their choices of areas of study. The current wave of careerism takes its toll because universities are not standing *together* to resist it, and they are individually incapable of such resistance. Supporting "nonproductive" (meaning underutilized) personnel is a presumed luxury that few will be permitted to enjoy. In this hasty capitulation to sometimes educationally unsound consumer demands, many colleges and universities are doing a disservice to their own students and faculties, and, additionally, often are failing American society itself.

The university's role as social critic has been collapsing under the pressures of short-run solutions undertaken in the name of institutional survival. Everywhere we are being asked to amputate and reduce in order to stay alive. But in the same way that we have come to learn the sorrows of "peace at any price," so too we may learn that survival at any price may be too high a price. If, however, there were sufficient statesmanship and cooperative action in the world of higher education, it might be possible to rally enough wisdom and public support to challenge some of the meaner-minded survival shibboleths and to return the university to its true mission: the creation of new knowledge and the stockpiling of old. Surely it is worth some effort.

Responding to the *Yeshiva* Decision
I. Michael Heyman

Since the *Yeshiva* decision, at least some part of the academic community and several unions have been preoccupied with the meaning of the decision as precedent. The literature already developed on the issue is considerable, and growing. Various conclusions have been drawn, including two obvious ones: First, the decision spells the curtailment of faculty collective bargaining in private higher education. And next, the decision solves problems for those administrators and trustees who disfavor faculty collective bargaining. I believe both conclusions are incorrect.

I agree with those observers who say there is too little history from which to draw conclusions. However, I also believe the conclusions drawn so far are important, not alone for what they say, but for what they miss.

Conceptions and Misconceptions

One important element in the Supreme Court decision was that the Yeshiva faculty members were management because they participated in a "mature" academic senate. What seems to be meant by a "mature" senate is one which is inextricably involved in or dominates academic decision making. Probably not many academic senates in our private colleges and universities meet this test, and even fewer in the public sector would do so apart from a number of the research universities. Often senates are felt to serve consultative roles in the best of times and something less than that otherwise. Indeed, as my colleague at Berkeley, Joseph Garbarino, one of the leading scholars in academic collective bargaining, stated: "The Court's account of faculty power at Yeshiva may lead some administrators to conclude that they would prefer to have their faculty unionized than to permit them to exercise the degree of authority claimed for the Yeshiva faculty."[1] In any event, I believe the *Yeshiva* decision probably will prove to have limited application.

Another conclusion drawn by some is that, though the *Yeshiva* case involves a private university—covered only by the National Labor Relations Act—it will have a precedential effect on the public sector. Some advocates of collective bargaining are depressed by this prospect; their opposites cheer. I believe both should pause. First, state legislatures are not looking for ways to limit collective bargaining; they are extending it.

In California, for example, the legislature in 1978 passed the Higher Education Employees Relations Act (HEERA), effective as of July 1, 1979, covering all academic ranks in the University of California system, the California State University and Colleges system, the Lawrence Livermore and Lawrence Berkeley laboratories, and the Hastings College of Law. Through HEERA, the

1. Joseph W. Garbarino, "Faculty Unionization: The Pre-*Yeshiva* Years, 1966–1979," *Industrial Relations*, Spring 1980, p. 228.

legislature was not looking for a way to block collective bargaining for faculty members; rather, a means to provide it was sought. That legislation, by the way, is unique. It makes specific provision for a bargaining unit of academic senate members and carves out the matters—largely academic—to be reserved to the academic senate. It thus seeks to limit the scope of bargaining largely to economic issues. This provision is interesting in light of the *Yeshiva* case, because it addresses directly the central issue in that case. Should faculty members be precluded from bargaining collectively on economic issues because they dominate academic decision making? The California legislature has said no by recognizing faculty in two defined capacities—as masters of the academic realm and as employees.

Second, the decision by the Supreme Court in *Yeshiva* cannot be viewed as the last word on the matters involved. Other tests will emerge, and the decision will be used as much by faculties with weak senates to argue for collective bargaining as it will be used by institutions with mature senates to argue against it.

Finally, some conclude that the *Yeshiva* case has "solved" the problem by limiting faculty collective bargaining opportunities. I suggest, however, that if many faculty members feel a need for collective bargaining, then the problem is whatever is causing these faculty members to feel that they are not properly accommodated in the sharing of decisions in academic governance or personnel. Limiting collective bargaining will not solve the problem; it will only create need for another alternative. And perhaps when compared to some alternatives, collective bargaining may be viewed as a conservative instrument.

Who Shapes Responses to Faculty?

Many faculty members, it seems clear, are less and less sanguine about their environment and working conditions. There are problems, stress, and negative perceptions. More and more layoffs are being contemplated, even among tenured faculty. There is a general decline in resources available to higher education; there is resentment among some publics to the whole notion of universities. Academic governance is being severely affected, if not often directed, by governmental regulatory agencies and compliance bodies. As universities grow and expand, they also consolidate and become systems with a seemingly remote "central administration" where, many faculty members presume, countless and increasing numbers of bureaucrats are conspiring to limit faculty prerogatives even further. Students are becoming more and more consumer-conscious and making demands on faculty for performance, quality controls, and participation in governance. State legislators today view their deep involvement in the detail of university programs as a legitimate activity.

These problems—and I have enumerated only a few—generate frustration, if not fear, in many faculty members. The problems need to be addressed.

If faculties believe collective bargaining will restore some of the environmental qualities previously associated with teaching and research in higher education, they will pursue it if there is no alternative. Indeed, some faculties believe collective bargaining will *create* status, rather than restore it. Carlene Clark, in a position paper on what the *Yeshiva* decision means for the University of California, wrote that "Bargaining in institutions with weak or no shared governance traditions has tended to create rather than to threaten faculty consultation rights."[2]

Let me use the University of California, Berkeley, where I am chancellor, to illustrate some considerations in collective bargaining and faculty-administration relationships. In May 1980, the members of the Academic Senate at Berkeley voted 532 to 477 against having an exclusive representative outside the senate for purposes of collective bargaining. The tally was announced on June 3, 1980. I'm not sure the Berkeley vote means as much as some people believe; it has raised as many questions as it has provided answers, not unlike the *Yeshiva* decision. The Berkeley senate is, by all the definitions used in the *Yeshiva* case, a "mature" senate; indeed, as far back as 1964, the Berkeley senate was referred to in the *AAUP Bulletin* as being "generally regarded as the most powerful such institution in the country." Yet the Berkeley senate members became one of the first faculties, from among the traditional fifty major research universities, to seek a vote on collective bargaining. As in the case with the *Yeshiva* decision, we can speculate on what this action meant. Probably, the special provisions of the California law (which seeks to protect the status of the Academic Senate by limiting the scope of bargaining) make the Berkeley vote less dramatic than it would have

2. Carlene Clark, "The *Yeshiva* Case: What Does It Mean for the University of California?" processed (Berkeley: University of California, May 1980), p. 12.

been were the institution operating under a statute less protective of the Academic Senate, say, other state statutes or the NLRA.

While I will not offer any guidelines, I suggest that if many members of the most powerful academic senate in the nation feel a need for structured dialogue on economic issues and a direct voice in the state capitol, the administration should examine with them the areas where they feel that faculty participation is weak and seek ways to strengthen it. As to a general approach, I urge enhanced collegiality. We must continue to enhance consulting with our faculty members and sharing decision making with them. The alternative is a continual quest for more rigid and formal systems such as collective bargaining.

Coping with a Deunionized Faculty Through Governance and Leadership
Walter Jewell

Yeshiva: Cataclysm, Armageddon, the Destruction of Faculty Power: no. The Triumph of Administration, Victory for Management, Unfettered Control: also no. Violent reaction, union and institutional, to the *Yeshiva* decision handed down on February 20, 1980, and predictions of dire consequences have not come to pass. The fall 1980 semester opened at colleges and universities affected directly by the decision without the crises forecast in the post-*Yeshiva* jeremiad. The ponderous mechanisms of the National Labor Relations Board have not produced reversals of refusals to bargain by independent colleges following the *Yeshiva* findings. Several NLRB regional directors have ruled that faculty members endowed with managerial authority are not entitled to bargain collectively. Investigations and hearings into alleged unfair labor practices will continue. The NLRB has decided to pursue a case-by-case determination of the facts with respect to independent colleges claiming status analogous to *Yeshiva*.

The effects of *Yeshiva*, however, transcend the narrow legal argument and the outcome of individual cases. *Yeshiva* gives cause for all actors in the drama of higher education to reflect on their duties and responsibilities as well as their rights. *Yeshiva* requires examination of the nature of organizational relationships in higher education and of how to improve those relationships. *Yeshiva* indicates that stresses between faculty and administration are real and that they require remediation if higher education is to do its duty well. *Yeshiva* provides an opportunity to create and strengthen academic governance and conflict resolution mechanisms beyond the borrowed rhetoric and rigid formulas of the industrial work place.

The Cataclysm That Didn't Happen

The cataclysm didn't happen, at least on one campus, my own, the University of New Haven, which elected to invoke *Yeshiva* and declined to continue bargaining with its faculty union. I should point out that from the union perspective, I am one of the bad guys, an administrator.

When the university's senior administrators examined the text of *Yeshiva* and evaluated its findings with respect to our situation, we were fully aware that *Yeshiva* was not carte blanche to spurn the faculty. Although we reasoned that the extensiveness of faculty authority would justify cessation of collective bargaining, we were well aware that *Yeshiva* rested on, and required, significant exercise of faculty authority in the affairs of the institution.

We saw the implications of *Yeshiva* as more than an excuse to escape the constraints of collective bargaining and the emotional costs of an adversarial bargaining relationship. We all strongly felt that bargaining *at our institution* was an inappropriate model for handling faculty-administration relations. As a young university where we were dramatically improving the quality of our programs and our organization and were growing during a period of increasing external and demographic constraints, we saw our four years' experience with collective bargaining as producing a formalism and inflexibility that threatened the impetus vital to a dynamically changing institution.

Contract relations and bargaining were not serving as good conflict resolution mechanisms, as sophisticated labor-management relations should. We understood that the poor quality of union-university relationships was rooted in historical events and personalities unique to our institution, factors not likely to be changed soon. One important perception was that adversarial bargaining was weakening the traditional mechanisms of faculty authority, which we valued highly and which were a strength of our institution. We knew, of course, that stereotypes of faculty-administrative roles did not credit an administration's commitment to the mixed model of collegial authority.

Our decision within the administration to cease bargaining was motivated by a desire to reinforce collegiality, or, in the *Yeshiva* terminology, managerial authority of faculty. We hold to the definition of collegiality as shared authority and shared responsibility. We do not subscribe to the definition of managerial authority put forth by national officials of the American Federation of Teachers and others, a definition that would give total and unaccountable control to the faculty members.

Cessation of collective bargaining will not mean increased administrative power. Faculty members are entitled to participate in governance. Their welfare concerns are real and require effective mechanisms to deal with their concerns. In the aftermath of reaction to a decision to invoke *Yeshiva*, significant effort must be made to reinforce such mechanisms. We believe that a diverse institution requires a variety of mechanisms suited to different constituencies and differing problems. Such creativity would be possible outside the industrial model, which is ill-suited to a collegial environment and is severely limited in the logic of its approach and in its legalistic constraints.

Much of this reasoning was communicated to the faculty in the president's announcement on March 7, 1980. It explained that since faculty members had so much managerial authority and were therefore not covered by the National Labor Relations Act, the university would no longer bargain with the union, but would seek to establish constructive discussions with the faculty on welfare issues.

The storm broke. Anger, fear, and uncertainty emerged in a seeming maelstrom of rhetoric and dire prediction. The faculty would strike; they didn't. The union threatened that faculty would withhold grades; they didn't. The university would increase teaching loads and take fantastic punitive steps against the faculty; it didn't. The legal battle would bankrupt everybody; it hasn't and doesn't seem likely to. Students would flee to other campuses; the retention rate is up and admissions are steady.

By mid-October 1980 the university community was able, with the exception of some few persons, to congratulate itself on its response to the cataclysm that wasn't there. All in all, administrators, faculty members, and students acted in ways appropriate to that great purpose of higher education—to encourage open and free discussion, based on reason. The university resisted the temptation to respond in kind to the more extreme propaganda. Salary increases awarded in April 1980, retroactive to the beginning of the academic year, calmed fears of retribution. Merit awards that did not discriminate—as feared—against union supporters increased the university's credibility. Faculty refusal to follow dramatic rhetorical threats showed that professionalism and commitment to education surpassed partisan sentiment and also calmed student anxieties, which had been whipped up by union activists, including some from off campus. Tenure and promotion deliberations, previously a point of contention, concluded without incident and helped to restore a sense of normalcy.

In the fall of 1980, rebuilding began. The faculty senate created a joint faculty-administration task force to explore initiatives to buttress collegiality. The usual governance bodies are in place and working.

Much more lies ahead. Confusion about future legalities is real. The NLRB is conducting hearings on the union's unfair labor practice complaint that the university has refused to bargain. Most people on campus see legal action as complex and threatening. Administrative efforts to prove the university really means to manage its affairs collegially will be crucial to faculty morale. (The "constitutional crisis" idea persists because the union, before its certification and affiliation, had been the old constitutional welfare committee.) The university stands ready to have substantive interaction with the faculty on welfare matters but depends on faculty leadership and initiative to create a mechanism for dealing with welfare issues. Union supporters can be expected to resist such a move.

Lesson 1: *Variations on a Theme*

The implications of *Yeshiva* will not be uniform. My institution's decision was based on its own circumstances. For us, no further bargaining seemed the best course. But proponents of the benefits of bargaining—faculty members, professional union officials, and management-labor relations professionals—have an argument. Bargaining when competently conducted by both sides can clarify expectations, reduce sources of conflict, and facilitate conflict resolution. Although *Yeshiva* indicates that faculty with management authority in private schools are not subject to mandatory bargaining under NLRA and NLRB, institutions are free to enter into voluntary bargaining relationships.

In institutions with successful bargaining histories and with trained staff or good consultants for both union and management, bargaining may well continue. Institutions without these resources will probably cease bargaining or resist attempts at unionization. My discussions with persons at several independent institutions considering their post-*Yeshiva* position have suggested that comfortable, sophisticated bargaining relationships are relatively rare in their sphere. I gather that, as contracts expire, few independent schools will elect to continue bargaining.

The NLRB policy on *Yeshiva*-like situations is to make a determination in each individual case. Circumstances vary among campuses, and *Yeshiva* itself brooks interpretation. Varied rulings, rather than a single outcome, seem likely.

Lesson 2: *Consider Real Faculty Motivations*

Decision makers, in constructing post-*Yeshiva* faculty relationships, need to think carefully about the faculty's fundamental motivations. In *Yeshiva*, the faculty members claimed they had a right of self-interest as professionals, qualifying them to bargain for wages, hours, and conditions of work. The Court held that, as managers, they had a duty to implement the policies of their employers. This argument and the Court's finding emanate from labor law. Although the Court used time-honored models of academe for examining faculty power, it ignored questions of faculty motivation.

An important question emerges: Are faculty members motivated basically by professionalism or by economic rewards? Professional motivation in the classical sense requires commitment to the calling, to clients, and to public service. A more current sense defines "professional" as a coveted status designation valued for its prestige and rewards more than for its self-fulfillment.

The relative economic condition of the professoriate compared to other professions such as law and medicine is responsible for much faculty frustration and militance. The suggestion remains, however, that decision makers need to distinguish between desires for support of professional work and desires for rewards.

A specter lurks here, familiar to faculty and administrators but not often discussed openly. Search for power, union or administrative, may to some degree be motivated by narrow self-interest without regard for professional ideals or for professional responsibilities. Many academic contracts, like their industrial counterparts, concentrate on limiting work and maximizing reward or vice versa without regard to noneconomic commitment to students, to scholarship, or to public service, except perhaps as pious preamble. I realize that practitioners, who themselves have a personal stake in the process, avow that collective bargaining strengthens professionalism in the good sense. My reading of numerous contracts, however, suggests *quid pro quo* takes precedence over dedication to the calling.

Freedom from the logical and legalistic constraints of the bargaining table gives institutions opportunities to enhance professionalism through application of a broad range of motivational mechanisms. Professionalism of work should be rewarded; status seeking without duty well performed should be discouraged.

Lesson 3: *Diversity Should Be Nurtured*

Colleges and universities are complex organizations. Their organizational diversity responds to the broad array of tasks set for academe and is necessary to creativity. The logic of mechanistic systems, of which collective bargaining is but one manifestation, threatens this healthy diversity. Collective bargaining seeks formulas, universal solutions, and rigidly defined relationships. Sophisticated concepts of bargaining move beyond mechanisms. These processes, however, represent an ideal rather than the reality of most bargaining and most contracts. The certitude of the formula may be comforting, but is unlikely to stimulate the vibrant, innovative environment that is supposed to characterize academe.

Lesson 4: *Deal with Legitimate Faculty Concerns*

Faculty members have legitimate concerns. Even holding self-interest out of the picture, they have cause for worry. The inability of institutions to keep up with inflation, the demographics of college attendance, shifts in interest in disciplines, job security, the growth of bureaucratic control are all just causes for anxiety. These must be responded to by faculty and administration *working together*.

The cooperation necessary to successful adaptation is less likely to be achieved in an adversarial context. Failure to take up the *Yeshiva* message—faculty as managers must manage—would not only justify collective bargaining but also severely weaken institutional effectiveness. The best way to remove real anxiety is to include faculty members in meaningful decision making. Balance and accountability must be maintained: to treat faculty members as employees is to justify their acting as such. In this sense the implication of *Yeshiva* is clear. Trustees and administrators in independent schools must effectively include the faculty in the governance of their institutions.

The collegial-managerial model, so necessary to the vitality of higher education, will be much harder to achieve in colleges and universities under state control. In states that have authorized collective bargaining, that model is likely to remain the rule. A few more states are likely to pass enabling legislation. In all states, legislative and bureaucratic control of public institutions will continue to make shared governance difficult. Political pressures will continue to support individual campuses and, at the same time, will demand central controls based on so-called rational plans.

Although professional responsibility embodied in collegial governance systems will be difficult to achieve in state-controlled institutions, it will not be impossible to attain. Administrative leadership and responsible faculty management can strengthen collegiality. The morass of state government responds to initiative. Colleges and universities that run themselves well are likely to be allowed more autonomy than those that are run like the usual state agency.

Lesson 5: *Manage the Outside Constraints*

Bargaining under the NLRB and state labor relations boards has required elaborate personnel practices necessary to respond to legislation and administrative law. Everyone is familiar with the myriad influences—whether intended to achieve worthy social goals or designed to increase bureaucratic power—of government units and politically motivated groups. Although many complain that ours is a nation of political apathy, actualities suggest that we are a nation more political now than at any time in our history. No sphere of activity is immune from new political pressure, government interference, and judicial oversight. Higher education is a favorite target for these activities. Education leaders who understand the pressures and organize their activities to influence the trends in political, bureaucratic, and judicial activity will be valued highly. Passivity will contribute to the possible decimation of higher education.

The points discussed here contain lessons for everyone involved in the higher education enterprise. Trustees should reexamine the extent of their involvement. Rather than acting as sounding boards and legitimating bodies for administration, they should consider and control the proper dynamic balance of constituent parties. Administrators need to eschew issues of relative power and, instead, ask themselves what legitimate, as distinct from selfish, faculty concerns require remediation. The smart administrator will want to make use of faculty members' talents in facing the challenges of institutional management. Full implications of the role of the academic manager need to be understood and acted on. Faculty members should reassess their professional responsibility in relation to their personal interests. Students' voices should be heard. Each party needs to understand the legitimate interests of the other parties and the necessity for cooperation. All must understand that failure to exercise competent, responsible governance of the institution, especially as measured by political publics, will lead to loss of autonomy.

IV. PRESSURES ON HIGHER EDUCATION—SPECIAL CASES

AMERICAN INDIANS

American Indians' Problems in Higher Education
Dean Chavers

American Indians began enrolling in higher education on a large scale for the first time at the very end of the 1960s, following the start of financial aid programs for poverty students. From a total college enrollment of some 1,400 in 1963, their numbers grew to about 35,000 by 1977.[1]

But while this decade and a half saw a twenty-five-fold increase in Indian enrollment, Indians have encountered some tremendous problems in achieving success in college. Their estimated dropout rate nationally is 85 percent; they have a course completion rate of only ten hours per semester; they have a lower grade-point average than other undergraduates; and their average number of semesters to graduation is twelve rather than eight.[2] In addition, there is a large but unknown number of stopouts, and Indian students remain isolated on the college campuses and from the larger society, even through the doctoral level.[3] Some 60 percent of Indian college graduates major in one field, education, to the detriment of such fields as the sciences, engineering, and business.[4]

Clearly, progress can be made in improving outcomes for Indian students. Four types of factors that are known—or believed—to affect the success rate of these students offer some basis for exploration and recommendations.

1. Dean Chavers, *The Feasibility of an Indian University at Bacone College* (Muskogee, Okla.: Bacone College, 1979), pp. 86–89.

2. Ibid., pp. 96–97; U.S. General Accounting Office, *The Bureau of Indian Affairs Should Do More to Help Educate Indian Students* (Washington: GAO, 1977).

3. Dean Chavers, "Isolation and Drainoff: The Case of the American Indian Educational Researcher," *Educational Researcher*, October 1980, pp. 12–16.

4. GAO, *The Bureau Should Do More*; Shirley M. Malcom, Rayna Green, and Jean L. Kaplan, *Inventory of Projects and Programs in Science for American Indians* (Washington: American Association for the Advancement of Science, 1976).

Institutional Factors

Certain characteristics of higher education institutions per se lead to lack of success for Indian students. Many of these can, however, be controlled by administrators. An analysis of data gathered by Locke from ninety-seven colleges with Indian programs revealed significant differences between those institutions reporting high retention rates for Indian students and those reporting low retention rates.[5]

- High-retention institutions had a larger average number of Indian students than those with lower retention rates.
- High-retention institutions had a larger number of program and support components, including a degree program in Indian studies, departmental status for this program, remedial help for students, an Indian Educational Opportunity program, and a guidance counselor.
- High-retention institutions more often had Indian material in the curriculum.
- Low-retention institutions more often had an Indian EOP program.
- High-retention institutions were more often private colleges.
- High-retention institutions more often offered a four-year degree program or higher.
- High-retention institutions more often had an Indian advisory committee for their Indian program.

There are underlying reasons for these differences. As noted above, Indian students are isolated on the campuses, tending to interact more with each other than with non-Indians.[6] The achievement of a "critical mass" of these students apparently gives them a base for making social contacts and friendships to replace the close family ties many of them left when they entered college and, further, to form their own support networks.

While high-retention institutions had a larger average number of program components than low-retention institutions, further analysis revealed discernible patterns in the mix of components. The high-

5. Patricia Locke, *A Survey of College and University Programs for American Indians* (Boulder, Colo.: Western Interstate Commission for Higher Education, 1978); Chavers, *Feasibility*, pp. 48–52.

6. Howard M. Bahr, Bruce A. Chadwick, and Robert C. Day, *Native Americans Today: Sociological Perspectives* (New York: Harper & Row, 1972), passim. Also Jack O. Waddell and O. Michael Watson, *The American Indian in Urban Society* (Boston: Little, Brown, 1971), passim.

retention institutions tended not to have an Indian EOP program or remedial help, but did tend to have Indian material in the curriculum more often. Thus, it appears that the type of support service available is important. An Indian studies program or department helps the student make the transition from familiar material to unfamiliar material gradually.

The involvement of the local Indian community is important to retention and success and most often takes the form of an advisory committee. The very fact that the administration is willing to respond to the needs of the Indian community is apparently important in retention.

Structural Factors

Certain other factors in the way programs are formulated and institutions are structured lie to a large extent beyond control by administrators and trustees, but can be addressed by policy makers in Congress and in the federal service. Among these is the high concentration of Indian students in two-year institutions, which Olivas reports to be 67 percent.[7] This concentration, in turn, is associated with much of the high dropout rate characteristic of the national dropout or noncompletion rate for two-year institutions.[8] This concentration is also associated with other factors: poor student motivation, unclear career goals, and transfer from one college to another—all factors associated with higher dropout rates.

Since the average income of Indian parents is low—less than half the average income of all families—few Indian parents can contribute to their children's higher education expenses. One 1973 study found that 96 percent of Indian parents were expected to contribute less than $300 per year toward college costs, according to federal guidelines.[9] The Bureau of Indian Affairs (BIA) grants and scholarship program, designed to take the place of loans and parental contributions, has grown tremendously since 1970—by 1980 to some $34 million for about 20,400 students,[10] or about 55 percent of the

7. Michael A. Olivas, *The Dilemma of Access: Minorities in Two-Year Colleges* (Washington: Howard University Press, 1979).

8. Alexander W. Astin, *Preventing Students from Dropping Out* (San Francisco: Jossey-Bass, 1977).

9. U.S. Department of the Interior, Bureau of Indian Affairs, Indian Education Resources Center, *Higher Education Evaluation: Student Characteristics and Opinions* (Albuquerque, N.M.: The Center, 1973). [Hereafter "IERC."]

10. Senator Henry Bellmon, Remarks at the dedication of the W. W. Hastings Indian Health Service Hospital, Tahlequah, Oklahoma, August 29, 1980.

Indian students. The other 45 percent will undoubtedly rely on loans to meet part of their financial needs, with the probability that their dropout rate will rise.

BIA and tribal officials who are responsible for the higher education scholarship programs operate under strong pressures to make their limited funds reach the maximum number of students. Consequently, Indian students are often urged to live at home and attend a local public two-year college, rather than leave home to attend another type of institution that might be better suited to their needs. While this practice makes the funds reach more students, it affects retention unfavorably for two reasons: living at home is less conducive to retention than living on a campus; and students attending two-year colleges must transfer to complete their degrees, and transfer leads to higher dropout rates.[11] For purposes of retention, it is better for Indian students to live on a campus and become involved with the life of the campus, avoiding the isolation that leads to attrition.

Characteristics of Students

Indian students have certain characteristics that impede success in college and that to some extent can be controlled by administrators. The most outstanding characteristic of Indian college students is their tie to their tribes and their people. Even among Indian doctorate holders, for example, over 70 percent are currently working in an Indian-related occupation—in public schools, for tribal governments, for the federal government, and so on.[12] Further, a high percentage of Indian college students are different from other students in important ways: they speak a native or first language other than English and come from a reservation area,[13] and they have strong ties to their land, their culture, their language, their religion, and their societies.

I offer no judgments here about whether it is bad or good for these students to become part of the larger society or to maintain their way of life. The research evidence shows that overwhelmingly their work preference upon graduation is for employment in some Indian-related area, which most often is in service delivery, such as

11. Astin, *Preventing Dropping Out.*

12. Chavers, *Isolation.*

13. IERC, *Student Characteristics.*

education, health, social work, and economic development. With this fact in mind, it would seem futile for a college or university to have an Indian program and assume the Indian students upon graduation will not behave as members of their tribes. Yet relatively few colleges—about one-quarter of those with sizable Indian enrollments—have designed their programs deliberately with these differences and with tribal loyalty in mind.[14]

Indian students, in addition to being politically and culturally different from the mainstream student, are educationally different. Many, if not most, have had poor high school preparation or preparation that would ready them for vocational or technical careers rather than for a liberal arts education. About 65–80 percent score in the bottom quartile on the ACT or SAT examinations, and only about 8 percent score in the top third. About two-thirds of them report that their biggest problems in college are poor study habits and motivation to study, things they have not learned in high school.[15] Few of them have clear plans for the career field they want to enter upon graduation, and spend the first year or two years exploring a number of options. At this point, the lower-division years, if the students find little to challenge, engage, and involve them, they are likely to drop out.

Even the demographics for Indian students are different. They are in general older than other students, with about one-third being older than the traditional 18–22 college-age cohort.[16] About one-third are married and are trying college as a possible path to a better way of life.[17]

The typical Indian student, then, enters college with only vague goals in mind, from a noncollege track in high school, with little financial or emotional support from parents (who most often have not completed high school themselves[18]), and with a sense of isolation from the college environment itself.

---

14. Locke, *Survey of Programs*; personal communication with Leroy Falling, director, BIA higher education grants program, 1979.

15. Chavers, *Feasibility*, pp. 91, 93.

16. IERC, *Student Characteristics*; Chavers, *Feasibility*, pp. 91–93.

17. IERC, ibid.; U.S. Department of the Interior, Bureau of Indian Affairs, *Statistics Concerning Indian Education* (Washington: The Bureau, annual).

18. U.S. Department of Commerce, Bureau of the Census, *Census of the Population, 1970: Subject Reports, Final Report PC(2)-1F, American Indians* (Washington: Government Printing Office, 1973).

Experiential Factors

Indian students entering college will undergo experiences different from any they have had before. The experiences they have at institutions of higher education can largely be controlled by the adminstrators at these institutions. The great majority of them have been educated at reservation high schools where almost all the students are Indian, or in high schools in reservation border towns where there are many Indian students. Because the typical college enrolls relatively few Indian students, they are likely to remain isolated from the main part of the student body and campus life. Campus involvement includes living in dormitories, having strong interpersonal relationships with faculty members, participating in extracurricular and intramural activities, and performing some meaningful part-time work.

With their poor high school preparation, they are too often placed in a higher level of class work than they can handle. Intensive counseling and personal assessment—transcripts, test scores, and personal interests—are needed in order to place them at an appropriate level of work in appropriate classes. Special attention should go to assessing their competence in the English language, because many of them have limited ability in English. At the same time, placing them entirely in bonehead classes is stigmatizing and self-defeating. One of the best techniques is to find their best subject and place them at the freshman level in that subject, with any remedial work being done in other subjects. Of importance, they need to have some good grades from the beginning, but should not be placed across the board in classes that are too easy.

Guidelines

College administrators and trustees can take many concrete actions to help improve the success rates for Indian students.

- Set a goal of having a "critical mass" of Indian students on the campus, so that they can be supportive of each other.
- Offer a wide variety of carefully selected support services designed to help these students make the transition to college life.
- Incorporate Indian material into the curriculum, either through a separate program or into already existing courses.
- Involve the local Indian community in the program through an advisory committee or by other means.
- Four-year and private colleges should recruit more Indian students because relatively few Indians enroll in these institutions and

because Indians apparently experience better success here than in other types of colleges.

- Seek to avoid giving loans as part of the financial aid package when possible. Work-study jobs or scholarships are more desirable for retention.
- Where possible, have them live on the campus rather than at home or in off-campus apartments.
- Take their differences into account by designing curricula appropriate to their backgrounds, by planning cultural events for them, by adopting sports in which they excel (boxing, track, cross-country), and by providing them with intensive study in the English language and in reading.
- Provide means for them to clarify their personal career goals.
- Learn what interests a particular student, and build on that.
- Involve them in campus life—sports, extracurricular and intramural activities, meaningful work, dorm life, and strong faculty relationships.
- Avoid stigmatizing them by allowing them to become known as poor students, a consequence of steering them predominantly into bonehead classes, admitting them under lower standards than applied to other students, and by encouraging them to major in ethnic studies programs. At the same time, their test scores must be taken with a grain of salt, and greater emphasis must be placed on high school grades and other factors.

Working together, institutions of higher education can have a tremendous influence on the education of Indian people in the next decade. With only six American Indian dentists, two American Indian podiatrists, and very low levels of parity in almost all other professions,[19] the educational future of Indian youth can only be brighter.

Higher Education for Indians
Dean C. Jackson

The relationship between Native Americans and the federal government of the United States throughout their history has invari-

19. Native American Information Center, Bacone College, *American Indians in the Professions* (Muskogee, Okla.: Bacone College, 1980).

ably resulted in tragedy. The myriad sociopsychological and economic problems that plague the Native Americans today stem directly from these tragic relationships. As one example, education and how it has been used have, in fact, contributed to the dilemmas of the Native Americans. The sorry situation is recognized in the title *Indian Education: A National Tragedy—A National Challenge*; that the title belongs to a 1969 report of the Special Subcommittee on Indian Education of the United States Senate Committee on Labor and Public Welfare is all the more telling. Within the report itself, the description is even more explicit: "a national tragedy" or "mental genocide."

Higher education for Indians as I discuss it here calls upon my knowledge of the Navajos in their efforts to use education as a vehicle to turn tragedies into triumph. Further, I shall use Navajo Community College as a model to explain how the Navajos are addressing their numerous problems through higher education. It is hoped that NCC will become representative of other Indian efforts in higher education.

The Navajos are just beginning to enter higher education: in the fall of 1980, for the first time in its brief history, Navajo Community College had to turn away students because of a shortage of facilities. The Navajo Tribal Government first made higher education scholarships available to the Navajos in 1953. Even with the scholarships, the proportion of Navajos seeking higher education in relation to the Navajo population has been low. Although thousands of Navajo youths have received aid through the Navajo scholarships annually, a large percentage have dropped out of colleges and universities. The incredible attrition rate of scholarship recipients caused an investigation by the Navajo Tribe. A study initiated in 1965 through Arizona State University revealed two major findings: (1) Most Navajo college students were ill-prepared for college work. (2) Most Navajo college students could not cope with the cultural shocks.

As a result of these findings, the Navajo Tribe decided to establish on their own land a college that would address their own problems as identified in the studies. Thus, Navajo Community College was born in 1969 at Many Farms, Arizona, in a facility borrowed from the Bureau of Indian Affairs. Many people doubted that the Navajos were capable of running their own college.

Today, Navajo Community College is located at Tsaile, Arizona, on a 1,200-acre site that the Navajo Tribe allocated strictly for higher education. It has a $20 million main campus at Tsaile, a branch campus at Shiprock, New Mexico, and about thirty-five extension sites located throughout the 25,000-square-mile Navajo Nation.

Navajo Community College was the first Indian-controlled community college. Today, there are some seventeen to twenty tribally controlled community colleges in the United States. These colleges have formed a consortium in an attempt to address collectively the total Indian higher educational needs.

Programs

The educational program at Navajo Community College is determined by its educational philosophy, which says in part:

> If a community is to continue to grow and to prosper, each member of that society must be provided with an opportunity to acquire a positive self-image and a clear sense of identity. To do so, it is necessary for every individual to both understand and to respect his/her own culture and heritage. It is the special purpose of Navajo Community College to promote among Navajos an understanding of their unique heritage, language, history, and culture.

To develop education based on this philosophy, Navajo Community College is developing a strong Navajo and Indian studies (NIS) program. In fact, NIS's importance and emphasis at Navajo Community College makes this educational institution unique among colleges. The purpose of Navajo and Indian studies is to provide a foundation on which individual students at NCC can structure or build their education. One tenet of the Navajo philosophy of education is that learning begins with the individual. A person who knows little about himself or herself is at a great disadvantage in embarking on an educational pursuit. That person is without identity, without which it is almost impossible to gain self-confidence. Without self-confidence, it is impossible to pursue and achieve a difficult task such as education.

The premise of the Navajo and Indian studies is that, historically, formal education has been a mechanism for an elimination and replacement process: eliminating the very substance that makes a Navajo a Navajo, and an attempt to replace it with a language, values, and ways that are alien to the Navajo. This elimination and the imposition of values and ways of life are what is referred to as "mental genocide." It is an education without foundation. Anything without foundation lacks stability and will not endure.

The Navajos have participated in the education of the dominant society for more than a hundred years since the Treaty of 1868. A treaty provision stated that the ultimate purpose of education was to civilize and Christianize the Navajos. To achieve these purposes, Navajos were to give up their language, culture, and values. But the Navajos were completely unwilling to comply. Education of the Navajos in the last hundred years can thus be described as a constant and continuous struggle between the two prevailing cultures. The conflicts between the two cultures have been the main reason for the Navajo's passive participation in the education system of the dominant society. Passive participation spells low motivation, low achievement, dropouts, alienation, and all the other education problems of the Navajos. Passive participation in the dominant society's education throughout its history is caused by a lack of goals or unclear goals.

Today, the picture in Navajo education has changed. For example, the Navajo Tribal Council in March 1980 passed a resolution that it develop its own energy resources by 1990. This resolution provides clear incentive for Navajos to pursue education so that they can become responsible for planning, developing, and implementing the tribal mandate. Navajo Community College has established a committee to seek roles and ways for the college to address the tribal energy mandate.

The Navajos are convinced that education is crucial to them in the modern world. They are also cognizant of the inefficacy and wrongs done to them through education by the dominant society. Navajos realized that neglect and the deliberate attempt to exclude from their education the valuable body of knowledge contained in their culture has contributed heavily to their plight today. A different approach is needed in the education of the Navajos. Such an approach must provide an opportunity for Navajos to remain Navajos and at the same time provide them opportunities to acquire the knowledge and skills necessary to participate meaningfully in the political, social, and economic world of today's society. The approach would examine, contrast, and analyze the values, philosophy, and educational concepts of the two prevailing cultures in which the Navajos live so that they are aware and are better able to cope with the conflicts and contradictions they encounter. The approach must be honest about the past and present relationship between the Navajos and the dominant society so that Navajos can be knowledgeable and be prepared not to let past tragedies be repeated. Such awareness and knowledge can be achieved only through education.

In addition to Navajo and Indian studies, Navajo Community College has built a strong liberal arts program. NCC awards A.A., A.S., and A.A.S. degrees. Credits for most of NCC's courses, including most of the Navajo and Indian studies courses, are transferable to universities and colleges surrounding the Navajo Nation.

Types of Control

Navajo Community College is an entity of the Navajo Tribe through Tribal Resolutions CJY-87-68 and CN-95-68. The Navajo Tribal Council delegates its authority to the Navajo Tribal Advisory Committee, which in turn delegates to the Navajo Community College Board of Regents the responsibility for maintenance and operation of the college.

The Board of Regents operates under its Plan of Operation, like any other organization. It meets once a month or more frequently if necessary. The Board of Regents is made up of ten members. The chairman of the Navajo Tribal Council, the chairman of the Navajo Tribal Education Committee, and the president of the student body serve ex officio. Two members serve at large and may or may not be members of the Navajo Tribe. The Navajo Nation is divided into five agencies, each of which has one representative on the Board of Regents. Navajo Community College and other tribal entities submit names to the chairman of the Navajo Tribe, who makes selections to the board with the concurrence of the Advisory Committee of the Navajo Tribal Council.

Navajo Community College has set precedents in higher education for other Indians, but, more important, it has also established a precedent in Navajo education: For the first time in Navajo education, Navajos sat down to spell out their educational needs and goals and how the goals are to be achieved. The Navajo Community College concept has provided opportunity for a thorough assessment of Navajo education. It is an example of Indians assuming responsibility for their own affairs. Through the Navajo Community College concept, the Navajos realize that education is the only way for Navajo survival. But that education must be relevant and must be one that provides a mechanism for survival in the modern world.

Links with Other Institutions

Some members of the Tribally Controlled Community Colleges have bilateral arrangements with other colleges and universities.

This action was necessary to gain eligibility for certain federal funding and recognition for course credit transfers. Navajo Community College has no official link with any other college or university because it is fully accredited. NCC does have close working relationships with many colleges and universities in program development, course equivalency guides, and nontraditional education programs.

Many colleges and universities are looking to Navajo Community College as a source to recruit upper-division students. They are also looking to NCC for leadership in Navajo and Indian studies programs.

Funding Sources

Navajo Community College's major funding source has been from Public Law 92-189, which was passed in 1971. The funds provided under this legislation are appropriated to the Bureau of Indian Affair's budget and then are given to the Navajo Tribe and finally to Navajo Community College.

In 1978, Public Law 95-471 (Tribally Controlled Community College Act) was passed. Its major differences from the original Navajo Community College Act is its formula funding: The formula provides $4,000 for each FTE (full-time equivalent unit) generated by Indian students. The formula funding has reduced Navajo Community College funding 61 percent from FY 80 to FY 81. The total level of the congressional appropriation for all the participating colleges in PL 95-471 is such that it will ultimately mean reductions in educational programs and, thus, decreased educational opportunity for Indian students.

TCCC's Problems of Survival

All members of the Tribally Controlled Community Colleges depend on funds from the federal government for survival. As noted above, PL 95-471 provides formula funding for each college that meets the eligibility criteria established by the Bureau of Indian Affairs. It also provides training and technical assistance money for those colleges that are now only in a formative stage. The amount appropriated for fiscal year 1980–81 for all the participating members is totally inadequate: the appropriation is only $4.8 million for operation of many colleges. Navajo Community College alone must have at least $6.4 million to maintain its present program level. Obviously, member colleges must work collectively in a lobbying effort to obtain an adequate funding level to ensure their survival.

Despite the success that Navajo Community College and other colleges have had through PL 95-471, some indications are that if the federal government fails to appropriate a level of funding for growth and development of tribally controlled community colleges, it will once again add to the long list of tragedies for the Native Americans.

Indian Higher Education—
Ideas from Research
Patricia Porter McNamara

The pressures to serve American Indians in higher education may be typified by the title of a report by the Special Subcommittee on Indian Education of the U.S. Senate Committee on Labor and Public Welfare—*Indian Education: A National Tragedy—A National Challenge.*[1] The challenge is one that the nation, the federal and state governments, and educators are still struggling to meet. Descriptive statistics and research studies document the continuing existence of educational problems or—more euphemistically—educational challenges, although the scope of the situation is often blurred by the number of definitions of who is an Indian, by the variety of data collection procedures used to describe the educational status and achievements of American Indians, and by the tendency to report enormous statistical increases that often obscure less impressive numerical gains. A "400 percent increase over the past decade" may, for example, mean that twenty-five people have entered a field in which only five Indian professionals worked ten years ago.

The subcommittee report focused on Indian education at the elementary and secondary level, as have most studies of Indian education. The reasons for this focus are obvious: Unless students receive an adequate academic foundation and remain in high school to graduation, their chances of entering, succeeding, and persisting in college are poor. In the 1960s, few Indians attended college and, in fact, the Bureau of Indian Affairs did not adopt a curriculum in its

1. Special Subcommittee on Labor and Public Welfare, *Indian Education: A National Tragedy—A National Challenge* (Washington: Government Printing Office, 1969).

high schools that encouraged postsecondary training, either academic or vocational, until 1963. The subcommittee's conclusions regarding higher education were principally that the elementary and secondary schools needed to upgrade the academic preparation they offered students. However, they also noted the need for a better understanding by teachers, administrators, and counselors of Indian students' problems and needs; more programs that provided academic and emotional assistance; and more scholarships.

Indian college enrollments have grown since 1969, and colleges and universities have increasingly found that the pressures and challenges of Indian education are a concern of higher education. Some institutions have accepted this challenge and attempted to respond by providing services to assist Indian students; others excuse extraordinarily high attrition rates by explaining that the students just weren't academically or emotionally prepared for college life, and they continue to search for "qualified" students.

One great hope is that, by changing institutional policies and practices, administrators and trustees can create an environment more attractive to, productive for, and supportive of the aspirations of Indian students, faculty, and staff members. Past research suggests some kinds of changes that can help create such an environment, and ongoing research is exploring additional areas. Many questions remain unanswered, yet there is a sufficient base of information to encourage and direct institutional efforts to provide better service to Indian peoples.

Findings from Past Research

The statistics and research findings on American Indians show that Indian enrollments in postsecondary education have increased dramatically over the past decade; that Indian students drop out of college at disproportionately high rates compared with students in general; that Indian students who pursue a college degree must often cope with serious and troubling academic, financial, social, and cultural problems that tend to distract them from their educational goals and detract from their academic performance; and that Indian graduates tend to hold degrees concentrated in a few fields, notably education and social sciences.

Enrollment Growth

The recent growth in Indian participation in postsecondary education is illustrated by the numbers of persons who have received financial assistance through the Bureau of Indian Affairs (BIA) higher education grants program over the past fifteen years. In 1965, this program awarded grants to 1,178 students; in 1970, to 4,271 students; in 1975, 15,500 persons received grants; and, in 1980, the program supported 21,000 students.[2] National statistics on the racial-ethnic composition of student enrollments in higher education for fall 1976 suggest that the representation of American Indians and Alaska Natives was at parity with their representation in the nation's population and in the case of undergraduates exceeded parity.[3] While these national estimates have been questioned[4]—and they may be inflated—the data show that in growing numbers Indian students perceive higher education as a viable option and aspire to college degrees.

Attrition Rates

A look at estimated dropout rates for Indian students quickly reveals that access to higher education cannot be interpreted as educational equity. The number of Indian students may have grown since the president of a public college in South Dakota reported that, over the thirty-three years from 1925 to 1958, a total of 112 Indian students had entered the college he headed, but retention is as serious an issue now as it was then. He found that nine (8 percent) of these students had remained enrolled for twelve or more quarters.[5] Although national attrition rates for Indians are not available, the BIA estimated only a few years ago that about 10 percent of Indian students eventually earned a degree; the comparable HEW estimate for all entering freshmen was 54 percent. While estimates are at best educated guesses, the dropout rate for Indian students has been put

2. American Indian Policy Review Commission, Task Force Five, Indian Education, *Report on Indian Education* (Washington: Government Printing Office, 1976); Leroy Falling, director of postsecondary education, Bureau of Indian Affairs, Washington, D.C., telephone conversation with Dean Chavers, 1980.

3. Department of Health, Education, and Welfare, Office for Civil Rights, *Racial, Ethnic and Sex Enrollment Data from Institutions of Higher Education: Fall 1976* (Washington: Government Printing Office, 1978).

4. Dean Chavers, Letter to Paul Mertins, branch chief, Higher Education General Information Survey, National Center for Education Statistics, August 29, 1979; Patricia McNamara, "Introduction to the Background and Issues of American Indian Higher Education," MS (Los Angeles: Higher Education Research Institute, 1980).

5. W. W. Ludeman, "The Indian Student in College," *Journal of Educational Sociology*, March 1960, pp. 333–35.

at 75 percent by Sorkin, 79–93 percent by McDonald, and 85 percent by Chavers.[6]

All retention studies of Indian students show disproportionately high attrition. The General Accounting Office (GAO) determined that of all 351 BIA grant recipient freshmen entering any one of seven colleges in 1974, fewer than half (46 percent) returned to the same institution the following fall, compared with 61 percent of the non-Indian freshmen. While the proportion of nonreturning Indian students ranged from 44 percent to 73 percent among the seven colleges and universities, the study made no attempt to determine what differentiated the schools with comparatively high retention rates from those with very low retention rates.[7] A study made by Carney followed the 1975 freshman class at the University of Oklahoma, Norman. At the end of nine semesters, 69.5 percent of the Indian freshmen, compared with 51.5 percent of the freshman class, were neither enrolled nor had they graduated.[8]

Neither of these studies followed up students who withdrew from college to determine whether they transferred to another institution or considered their withdrawal to be temporary. The GAO study does report that the mean grade-point average of nonreturning freshmen was 1.4, slightly below a D+. This finding suggests that their eligibility for BIA financial assistance was forfeited and that their academic experience had been neither especially successful nor likely to encourage educational aspirations.

Educational Barriers

The barriers to educational persistence and achievement for Indian students are described in the research literature. In fact, the problems Artichoker and Palmer described twenty years ago have

6. Estimates from the Department of Health, Education, and Welfare, in U.S. Government Accounting Office, *The Bureau of Indian Affairs Should Do More to Help Educate Indian Students* (Washington: GAO, November 1977); Alan L. Sorkin, *The Urban American Indian* (Lexington, Mass.: Lexington Books, 1978); Art McDonald, "Why Do Indian Students Drop Out of College?" in *The Schooling of Native America*, ed. Thomas Thompson (Washington: American Association of Colleges for Teacher Education, 1978), pp. 73–85; Dean Chavers, *The Feasibility of an Indian University at Bacone College* (Muskogee, Okla.: Bacone College, 1979).

7. GAO, *The Bureau Should Do More.*

8. Myrna Carney, "Comparative Graduation and Retention Rates by Sex and Ethnic Background" (Norman: University of Oklahoma, Office of Student Affairs Research, 1979–80).

been documented over and over again: (1) poor academic preparation; (2) financial difficulties; (3) lack of a clear sense of purpose or
direction, especially in regard to educational and career goals;
(4) concern about moral and religious questions, a concern that the
authors do not explain but one that probably corresponds closely to
the problem defined by subsequent researchers as culture conflict;
and (5) family responsibilities.[9] These same problems were identified
by the 1969 report of the Special Subcommittee, which also pointed
out the often difficult emotional and social adjustment an Indian
student must make upon entering an environment with different
customs and values. McDonald has suggested that a lack of role
models negatively affects persistence, a problem closely related to
that of unclear goals and direction.[10]

Higher Education Evaluation stands out as remarkably innovative in a literature that tends to count students and examine academic records. The Indian Education Resources Center asked Indian
students what problems they had encountered and asked dropouts
why they withdrew from college; the survey instrument did supply
pre-coded responses. The problems most often cited by the 2,736 BIA
grant recipients were poor study habits (26 percent), inadequate
preparation for college (23 percent), lack of motivation to study (18
percent), lack of finances (15 percent), and lack of friends and
homesickness (7 percent). Twenty-eight percent of the survey respondents reported that they had dropped out of college in the past
year and most frequently indicated as their primary reason for this
decision: family obligations (21 percent), lack of funds (20 percent),
went to work (18 percent), and inability to see the relevance of their
course work (14 percent). [11]

The GAO study found that students with higher ACT scores
tended to earn higher college GPAs, and Patton and Edington report
that college GPA was the best predictor of student persistence for
Indians attending two New Mexico public universities. The findings
of two studies suggest, however, that the level of freshman academic

9. John Artichoker and Neil M. Palmer, "The Sioux Indian Goes to College"
(Vermillion: University of South Dakota, Institute of Indian Studies, 1959).

10. Special Subcommittee, *Indian Education*; McDonald, "Why Do Indian
Students Drop Out?"

11. *Higher Education Evaluation: Student Characteristics and Opinions*, Research and Evaluation Report Series, no. 20-A (Albuquerque, N.M.: BIA Indian
Education Resources Center, 1973).

preparation does not differentiate persisters from dropouts.[12] Kohout
and Kleinfeld found that Native students entering the University of
Alaska with high levels of academic preparation were succeeding at
a much lower rate than their non-Indian peers and that their rate of
success had not increased from 1962 to 1973. They also found that
the persistently high attrition rates for Native students could not be
ascribed to academic failure. The proportion of Native students
dismissed for academic reasons had declined from 57 percent in
1963–64 to 8 percent in 1971–72.[13] The GAO study found that the
average composite ACT scores for 351 Indian freshmen was 13, a
random sample of 430 Indian undergraduates was 14, and a sample
of 203 recent Indian college graduates was 14—almost identical—all
falling within the range considered indicative of a restricted educational development background.[14]

Culture conflict, often cited as a cause of the disproportionately
high attrition of Indian students, tends to be superficially described
in the context of the emotional and social adjustment that students
from rural, noncompetitive backgrounds must make when they
enter a strange new environment, the competitive urban campus
with its particular and—to the Indian student—different customs
and values.[15] McDonald reports that the reservation residents he
interviewed felt the high school to college transition was extremely
difficult because the entire campus environment and attitude were
alien to reservation students.[16] Ross discussed the dropout problem
with more than fifty Yakima Indians, all but five of whom felt that
the primary cause was the cultural strains students experienced on
college campuses. The Yakima live on a rural reservation, but two-
thirds of the reservation residents are non-Indians and most Yakima

12. GAO, *The Bureau Should Do More*; Walter Patton and Everett D. Edington,
"Factors Related to the Persistence of Indian Students at the College Level," *Journal
of American Indian Education*, May 1973, pp. 19–23.

13. Karen Kohout and Judith Kleinfeld, *Alaska Natives in Higher Education*
(Fairbanks: University of Alaska, Institute of Social, Economic, and Government
Research, 1974).

14. GAO, *The Bureau Should Do More*.

15. Ibid.; Special Subcommittee, *Indian Education*; *Review of the Literature on
Educational Needs and Problems of American Indians and Alaskan Natives 1971
to 1976*, Research and Evaluation Report Series, no. 64:00 (Albuquerque, N.M.:
Bureau of Indian Affairs, 1977).

16. "Why Do Indian Students Drop Out?"

students grow up speaking English and attending local integrated elementary and secondary schools.[17]

Ross explores the meaning and causes of culture conflict in depth through a case study analysis of Yakima cultural traits. She describes the task students face when they enter college as living in two worlds, worlds where the structure and importance of family, the meaning of prestige and how one acquires it, and the purpose and use of accumulated wealth are different. She defines culture conflict as "the result of situations in which behavior that is perceived as unintelligible or misleading by members of one cultural group is at the same time seen by members of another cultural group as acceptable and expected behavior arising from a coherent conceptualization of life."[18] Ross describes the cultural traits of the Yakima— many of which are shared by other Indian tribal cultures—and compares them with the commonly expected values and behaviors on most predominantly white campuses. The sources of misunderstanding, confusion, and strain for both Indian students and educators are evident.

Thus, the literature identifies and describes the problems of Indian students; on the other hand, insights into ways to facilitate educational achievement and persistence and ways to address successfully the needs and problems of Indian students are few and far between. Institutional evaluations of particular programs that provide precollege orientation, counseling, or academic assistance tend to show that Indian students who participate do benefit;[19] however, the students who choose to participate in these programs may well be a select group who would have persisted at higher rates or earned better grades whether or not these services were available. Frustrated by the lack of information about what works in Indian higher education, Chavers examined descriptive data compiled by Locke on Indian programs at ninety-seven colleges and universities.[20]

17. Kathleen A. Ross, "Cultural Factors in the Success and Failure of American Indian Students in Higher Education: A Case Study for the Yakima Indian Nation" (Diss., Claremont Graduate School, 1979).

18. Ibid., pp. 47–48.

19. Special Subcommittee, *Indian Education*; GAO, *The Bureau Should Do More*.

20. Dean Chavers, "What Works in Higher Education?" Syndicated column available from the author, Bacone College, Muskogee, Okla., 1980; Patricia Locke, *A Survey of College and University Programs for American Indians* (Boulder, Colo.: Western Interstate Commission for Higher Education, 1978).

He was able to identify seven differences between colleges reporting high and low dropout rates. However, an examination of his data source discloses tremendous variation in the attention given and the detail provided by respondents to the survey forms: some programs offer no estimate of their retention rate; some say "great" or "we try to retain all our Indian students"; some provide an estimated retention range (40–60 percent) or an approximate figure ("about half," "one-third"); and a few actually report data-based figures.

Fields of Study

Research and data on Indian students document another finding about their situation: Indian students are concentrated in a limited number of fields, especially education and social sciences. The GAO study found that of 189 recent Indian graduates, some of whom had earned associate degrees, 56 percent majored in education, 18 percent in sociology or psychology, 12 percent in business, 9 percent in liberal arts, 3 percent in sciences, and 2 percent in medical fields.[21] The distribution of Indian bachelor's degree recipients in 1975–76 by major field was compared with that of white students and showed 46.5 percent of the Indian graduates majored in education and the social sciences, against 38.9 percent of white students.[22]

Certainly Indian educators and social scientists are needed. However, to the extent that forces are at work that prohibit entry or exclude Indian students from engineering, mathematics, the sciences, business, medicine, and law, an inequitable situation exists and should be addressed. Proficiency in mathematics or, at the very least, a willingness to study mathematics is a prerequisite to entering almost all of these fields. Artichoker and Palmer, and *Review of the Literature*, already cited, specifically point to mathematics and the sciences as problem areas for Indian students. A college counselor reports: "The main problem areas for Native American students . . . are in math and sciences; physics, biology, chemistry, and computer sciences."[23] Green found math anxiety, math avoidance,

21. GAO, *The Bureau Should Do More*.

22. Department of Health, Education, and Welfare, Office for Civil Rights, *Data on Earned Degrees Conferred from Institutions of Higher Education by Race, Ethnicity and Sex, Academic Year 1975–1976*, vol. 1 (Washington: Government Printing Office, 1979).

23. *Evaluation Report on Indian College Student Counseling Program, University of New Mexico, New Mexico State University*, Research and Evaluation Report Series, no. 20-B (Albuquerque, N.M.: BIA Indian Education Resources Center, 1976), p. 24.

and inadequate preparation in mathematics to be the most pervasive and serious barriers to success in general education and to the selection of scientific and technical career goals,[24] as did participants in the Conference on Mathematics in American Indian Education.[25] Until more is known about ways to create interest and build skills in mathematics, few Indians will enter such fields as engineering, where it is estimated that 4,500–5,700 Indian engineers are needed before Indian representation will be at parity with the representation of Indians in the nation's population.[26]

Current Research Projects

Several studies in progress promise to add to the knowledge about Indians in higher education, and undoubtedly there are other ongoing studies with which the author is not familiar. Researchers at the University of New Mexico, funded by the Carnegie Corporation of New York, are finishing a reference directory of higher education programs for Hispanic Americans and American Indians. The directory will be of particular value to high school and college counselors and students who wish to identify and compare programs and assess the availability of institutional and community support services for Indian students.

"Tracking of Higher Education Students Supported under the Indian Education Act," a follow-up of all students who have received funding from the Department of Education's Office of Indian Education (OIE) since 1976, is being conducted by Native American Research Associates (Lawrence, Kansas). Some 350–400 Indian undergraduate and graduate students who have received support through the Indian fellowship program as well as 2,500–3,000 students, mostly undergraduates and some non-Indian, who have participated in the Educational Personnel Development Program will receive a questionnaire inquiring about their background, educational experience (institution[s] attended, major field, degree

24. Rayna Green, "Math Avoidance: A Barrier to American Indian Science Education and Science Careers," in *Report and Recommendations: Conference on Mathematics in American Indian Education*, ed. Rayna Green, Janet Welsh Brown, and Roger Long (Washington: American Association for the Advancement of Science, 1978), Appendix D.

25. Green, Brown, and Long, ibid.

26. Paul Greenbaum, Al Becenti, M. M. Cole, and C. Wishkeno, "The Number and Need for Native Americans in the Designated Professions," MS (Lawrence, Kan.: Native American Research Associates, 1980).

completion status, and financial aid), and current job. The primary purposes are to establish a student data system for OIE and to determine whether the intent of the legislation is being carried out: Are students completing their degrees? Are they being trained in the mandated areas? Are they working in positions where they serve Indian people?

The Higher Education Research Institute (the organization with which I am associated) is engaged in a national assessment, supported by the Ford Foundation, of the progress over the past decade toward educational equity for the four groups most underrepresented in higher education: American Indians, blacks, Chicanos, and Puerto Ricans. The dimensions of this task have dictated a multifaceted research design, only one component of which I shall pursue here as related to higher education for Indians—a study of the experiences and perceptions of Indian faculty members, counselors, and administrators.

Research Findings Suggest Institutional Changes

Of 150 Indian educators who received the first-phase open-ended survey form for the HERI study, 94 (63 percent) responded and the wife of one respondent also answered our questions. These respondents reside in twenty-one states and the District of Columbia and represent fifty-one colleges and universities, including seven predominantly Indian colleges; eight two-year colleges; thirty-eight public, seven private, four tribally controlled, and two federally supported institutions. Their information is especially valuable because they are Indians working with Indian students in higher education institutions and because, despite the barriers to educational achievement, they have succeeded in the world of academe.

All but two of the Indian educators had earned bachelor's degrees; 84 percent held graduate or professional degrees. Of the 39 doctoral degree recipients and candidates, 28 percent had earned their degrees in education and seven were in more quantitatively oriented fields—three in biological sciences and one each in chemistry, economics, environmental health, and physical geography. Almost two-thirds (64 percent) of the respondents were men and one-third were under age thirty-five. Their entry into the academic world corresponds to the advent of pressures to increase minority participation in higher education: 85 percent reported their first academic appointment occurred after 1965, and 29 percent did not accept their first academic job until 1976 or later. The recency of their entry into academe is reflected in their position on the tenure-track ladder. Of the 58 who reported a faculty title, two-thirds were instructors, lecturers, and assistant professors, and only five had attained the rank of full professor. Almost one-third reported that they administer programs for Indian students, which, for many, is a responsibility they combine with teaching.

One area about which very little is known is what the experience of working in colleges and universities is like for minorities. The vast majority (86 percent) of the Indian educators felt that they face particular problems related to the fact that they are Indian; most of those who reported no special problems worked in predominantly Indian colleges. These respondents indicated that they find themselves working—often alone—to counteract stereotypes, ignorance, and misconceptions about themselves, Indian students, and Indian cultures and communities; serving as *the* voice for all Indians on countless committees and as *the* advisor to Indian and often other minority students; defending their own academic credentials, the academic merit of Indian studies, and the importance and value of research into concerns outside the traditional scholarly purview; and having the time and energy they devote to serving the institution and its students ignored in promotion decisions.

The six problems most often mentioned by respondents who listed special problems related to their "minority" status are summarized below:

- Gaining the acceptance and respect of colleagues: disproving the assumption that Indians are less competent (32 percent);
- Working in an environment characterized by ignorance and insensitivity to the perspectives, values, and customs of Indian cultures and Indian students and the capacity of both to enrich the academic curriculum and environment; having constantly to educate faculty and administrators (27 percent);
- Isolation and overwork: the lack of other minorities to do all the work that needs to be done, to serve as advocates for and advisors to minority students, and to develop a support network among themselves (20 percent);
- A promotion system that ignores time- and energy-consuming involvement in minority affairs, involvement that is often expected or required by the institution (17 percent);
- Being stereotyped as the minority or Indian "expert"—the profes-

sional consequence of which is often getting stuck in a job with limited opportunity for advancement to more broad-based and influential positions (15 percent); and

- Lack of support and recognition for teaching and research in Indian studies courses, programs, and about Indian issues (15 percent).

These and other less frequently mentioned problems are not beyond the control of institutional administrators and trustees, nor can they afford to ignore them. Although these respondents are determined and committed persons, several have decided that they no longer have the energy or the faith necessary to continue working in higher education. Colleges and universities that have sought and hired Indian faculty and staff members have indeed taken a positive and affirmative first step, but now these institutions must support these persons, recognizing and attempting to alleviate the pressures and demands they experience.

The three recommendations most frequently offered by these educators about what colleges and universities can do to better serve Indian students suggest institutional changes that would benefit students and also improve the institutional climate for Indian faculty and staff members. One-fourth of the respondents urged institutions to recruit and hire additional Indian faculty, counselors, and administrators and to work at retaining and promoting those they currently employ. One recent Ph.D. explained: "They should recruit Indian faculty members to serve as examples [role models], but mainly because they can relate to and advise young upcoming Indian scholars. Indian college students are more apt to trust and confide in Indian faculty members rather than the most sincere non-Indian faculty members."

A suggestion made equally often is that an appreciation for, and understanding of, Indian culture and values be promoted throughout the campus, but that special attention be given to educating the educators and counselors who interact with Indian students. One respondent suggested that a curriculum on the Indian culture of the region be developed for people going out to make contact with Indian young people. "Promote an understanding of the race as one having a heritage that is significant and important," advises one faculty member. Another proposed that colleges sponsor Indian cultural activities, such as pow-wows, art displays, and lectures by noted Indian personalities, and encourage *all* students to attend. A third contended that higher education institutions must work to relieve the institution of the stereotypes of Indians that now prevail and to relieve the Indian communities of stereotypes they hold about themselves, presumably meaning such misconceptions as "Indians can't succeed in higher education" or "Indian students aren't able to do mathematics." One respondent wrote, "Native American culture and white culture [non-Indian] have highly divergent values systems. Often the educational institution is unaware of exactly what differences really exist or, if aware, is unwilling to deal with the differences in constructive and creative ways."

About one-fifth (21 percent) of the educators emphasized the importance of establishing and supporting Native American studies courses, programs, or departments as a stable part of institutional offerings, that is, of ending the reliance on "soft" money and the annual uncertainty about their continued existence. One advocate for the support of Indian studies programs explained: "They offer a great potential for enrichment of the general education curriculum and specific philosophical wealth that has aided in the survival of so many tribes." Another distinguished professor suggests that strong Native American studies programs be developed within each public system of higher education, although not necessarily on every campus, and that students be guided to these key centers; he added: "Indian students should *not* go to those colleges that have no Indian faculty on hard money."

"The financial problems faced by every Native American student are so horrendous and create such great obstacles that they defeat many persons attempting to enter college." About one-fifth (19 percent) of these educators spoke about the need for institutions to provide adequate financial aid counseling and support, including ensuring that students receive their aid on time. Many students have little experience in managing money; some attempt to send home to their family some part of a stipend that barely meets their own needs. Although institutions often assume that the federal government supports Indian students' financial needs, many students cannot meet the eligibility criteria for federal grant programs, nor are the grants necessarily adequate to meet the students' needs.

Sixteen percent of the respondents encouraged colleges and universities to work with Indian communities to identify and to provide technical assistance or programmatic responses to educational, manpower, and research needs. "Lend support to the development of community-based educational programs and provide various forms of technical assistance, as requested, to help Indian nations pursue self-determination in education on their own reservations," recommended one educator. An additional 9 percent specifically urged colleges to become actively involved in improving the elementary and secondary schools attended by Indian students. Three other faculty members suggested that cooperative and internship programs be developed so that Indian students can serve their communities while they're in school.

The need for outreach and recruitment efforts, a renewed commitment to affirmative action, the adoption of a multicultural approach within the standard curriculum ("Adopt a holistic approach to all topics. If you're going to teach government, don't confine it to Western Europe.") and for strong remedial and academic support services were each mentioned by 15 percent of the Indian educators. Another 12 percent each emphasized the importance of offering strong academic, career, and personal counseling and of providing special support services and programs, including student organizations and meeting places. One young respondent said of his own undergraduate experience: "I would not be here today if it wasn't for a support program such as . . . . Community support, staff support, peer group support, and family support all worked together."

This partial list of Indian educators' recommendations to higher education institutions suggests a number of areas where colleges and universities can assess their current efforts and a number of ways in which they can better serve Indian students. Indian students are as heterogeneous in background as any other group of students. Nonetheless, many have or are seeking to develop an identity with Indian tribal cultures that differ greatly from the culture reflected in the values and expectations of the nation's colleges and universities. From the missionary beginnings of Indian higher education, Indian students have been perceived as "disadvantaged" and as culturally and academically "deficient." Now we must learn to recognize their talents and strengths and provide the support and services they need to develop in the directions they choose for themselves. Higher education institutions can better serve Indian students, explains one respondent, by realizing "that *they* have to adapt to the students' *legitimate* needs—in terms of offering pertinent courses, developing a minimum number of students from that group at the institution, and permitting internship and leave-term experiences that don't force a student to choose between his or her home community and an academic setting in any final way."

ENHANCING PRODUCTIVITY

Surviving in the 1990s—
Increase Productivity in the 1980s
Eldon G. Schafer

In turbulent times, Peter Drucker points out, survival has priority. To that end, colleges and universities have been discovering something usually neglected on campuses: productivity means doing more with less. Drucker makes the challenge clear: raise productivity at least 50 percent in the 1980s without employing more people. To do so means increasing employee output at an annual rate of 4–5 percent. Can it be done? Drucker insists that the only obstacle is hard work. In any event, this decade cannot be as easy for us in academe as for manufacturers of insulation, long underwear, or small cars.[1] When I note, however, that virtually every institution of higher education is doing something to enhance productivity, I am optimistic. We can be more productive because we and our institutions are like tea bags: we don't know our own strength until we get into hot water.

Resources for Suggestions
The meaning of "productivity" for academia will probably vary among institutions as each looks at its specific needs and challenges. A starting definition is offered by Clarke, who suggests that productivity "is increasing the quantity and quality of learning and personal growth while being cost effective." Community colleges have defined productivity according to achievements in seven operational elements, some of which seem equally appropriate for four-year institutions: (1) increase the learning of students; (2) help the staff become more efficient; (3) make the community college more accessible to a wider range of students; (4) lower the cost of producing a unit of education; (5) reduce attrition rates; (6) develop and

1. Drucker, *Managing in Turbulent Times* (New York: Harper & Row, 1980), pp. 1, 20; and Susan C. Nelson, "Future Financing and Economic Trends," *Community and Junior College Journal*, September 1980, p. 42.

implement a more efficient administrative organization; and (7) manage facilities and resources more effectively.[2]

I suspect that, to managers, the last two represent the least difficult challenge and probably are the areas in which chief productivity gains have been realized thus far. Gaining staff cooperation for an activity such as energy saving and then measuring the saving is far simpler than "helping the staff become more efficient" and quantifying that achievement.

Many truly outstanding efforts in resource and facilities management have been recognized and chronicled since about 1975 through the Cost Reduction Incentive Awards program of the National Association of College and University Business Officers (NACUBO) and the U.S. Steel Foundation. Winners of $10,000 awards in recent years have included Lane Community College (the institution with which I am associated) for cutting electrical usage in half and saving $100,000 a year;[3] Creighton University for an employee suggestion system that elicited creative ideas that saved the institution $124,000 in one year; Daytona Beach Community College for plant energy savings of $37,000 in one year; and Skidmore College for using waste automotive oil in its boilers to save $234,000 in one year. Information about more than a hundred exemplary programs can be secured by writing NACUBO. An additional resource relating solely to energy projects at some fifteen colleges is "Energy Management in the Community College: The Projects and Personnel," prepared by the League for Innovation in the Community College.[4]

Goodwin and Young summarize a number of experimental activities relating to enhanced performance by administrators, faculty, and students. Activities have ranged widely and included information management systems, differentiated staffing, new forms of instruction, grading systems, and learning styles. Priest and

2. Johnnie Ruth Clarke (Paper delivered at the Conference on Increasing Productivity in the Community College, League for Innovation in the Community College, Charlotte, N.C., October 31–November 2, 1977); and League for Innovation in the Community College and the Dallas County Community College District, "A Proposal to Establish the Community College Productivity Center," Paper (Los Angeles, Calif.: n.d.), p. 3.

3. Paul Colvin, "Energy Management: The Success of a Seven Year Program at Lane Community College," Paper (Eugene, Ore.: March 10, 1980). Write to LCC, 4000 E. 30th Ave., 97405.

4. Write to NACUBO, attention of Debi Bird, One Dupont Circle, Suite 510, Washington, D.C. 20036. Write to LICC, 1100 Glendon Ave., Westwood Center, Suite 925, Los Angeles, Calif. 90024.

Pickelman detail similar efforts in the Dallas Community College District.[5]

This list of productivity efforts merely scratches the surface of the known and scarcely known. I believe there are endless stories to be shared, to our mutual gain. Productivity includes avoidance of time spent reinventing the wheel; hence, the importance of reviewing what other institutions are doing and adopting or adapting. I know of no one document that catalogues and classifies such activities at all types of colleges and universities across the nation. If there is a grant out there in search of a constructive and potentially fruitful project, the catalogue could be it. The institutions need some broadly inclusive "yellow pages" of productivity to help publicize models and stimulate thinking.

Gaining Support for Productivity Activities

Exchanging ideas, methods, and encouragement has been effective through consortia as well as on a one-to-one basis. As one example, the League for Innovation in the Community College and the Dallas (Texas) County Community College District have established a National Community College Productivity Center. Now in the second year of a three-year $263,100 grant from the Carnegie Corporation of New York, the center is working with some sixteen institutions on sixty projects. Efforts include increasing staff utilization by 5 percent, reducing energy use by 5 percent, and reducing student attrition by 5 percent.[6]

Building on the beginning made by the National Productivity Center, Lane Community College now has its own campus productivity center. A $5,000 Development Fund allocation provided start-up monies. We hope to raise the visibility of what is being achieved, stimulate better performance, and coordinate ongoing efforts in the various departments. The center's coordinator reports to the president, thus conveying clearly that the president intends productivity to be a central function of the college. I doubt that broad enhance-

---

5. Gregory Goodwin and James C. Young, "Increasing Productivity in the Community College," Topical Paper, no. 67, ERIC Clearinghouse for Junior Colleges (Los Angeles, Calif.: ERIC, July 1980); and Bill J. Priest and John E. Pickelman, *Increasing Productivity in the Community College* (Washington: American Association of Community and Junior Colleges, 1976).

6. Write Community College Productivity Center, 701 Elm St., Dallas, Tex. 75202.

ment of productivity can occur without presidential commitment and participation.

Staff development is central to the operation, since people (whose salaries take 80 percent of our budget) are our most readily available resource. Productivity of people requires continuous learning, Drucker reminds us: "One learns in order to do better what one already knows how to do well." Key assistance in developing our program has come from the North American Consortium for Staff Development at the University of Texas.[7] Given the widely publicized changing nature and expectations of today's workers, the center at Lane is also seeking self-organizing, self-adaptive, participative approaches to enhancing productivity. Though Lane has strong unions on campus, I am convinced that management and staff will come together on issues of survival, as was demonstrated during the local property tax funding elections. At least one study nationally indicates the same kind of cooperation is possible on campuses. Yankelovich reported that almost all managers and union officials agreed with the statement "It is possible for the union and management to cooperate on specific programs which will improve productivity."[8]

While change isn't for many people, I take heart in the reminder from Boyd that "the very purpose of education is to induce change." Abba Eban, Israeli statesman, spoke of a larger sphere but offered advice that might help us see our situation as workable: "If I am optimistic, it is because I believe men and nations do behave reasonably after they have exhausted all other alternatives."[9]

Managing for Productivity

Of course, changes cannot be confined to faculty and staff alone. Managers, too, must learn better the pragmatic warning of Deutsch to "communicate or litigate." Avoidance of litigation is also a form of productivity. Managers, in particular, must retrain themselves to

7. Drucker, *Managing*, pp. 24–25. Write to NACSD, Educational Administration Division, Ed. B. 348, University of Texas, Austin, Tex. 78712.

8. Quoted by John W. Kendrick, "Increasing Productivity," in *Inflation and National Survival*, ed. Clarence C. Walton (New York: Academy of Political Science, 1979), p. 202.

9. William Boyd, "Dispelling the Post-Partum Blues," in *Addresses and Proceedings* (Oakland, Calif.: Western College Association, 1980), p. 10; Eban, quoted by William Gerberding, "Apocalypse Later," in *Addresses and Proceedings*, p. 20.

Think Productivity. This step may require, as Kastens states, the abandonment of the standard definition of management—"getting things done through and with others." He insists the definition can apply to mismanagement and aimless busywork. Kastens offers a tougher, results-oriented definition of the manager's job: "A manipulation of available resources in such a way as to create something of value that did not exist before."[10] The new definition describes a proactive manager, one who makes things happen, whereas the reactive manager waits for things to happen. Productivity requires the new kind of manager.

Changes in priorities are required. Managerial time must be shifted from less productive work. Resources must be concentrated on results, Drucker insists: feed the opportunities and starve the problems.[11]

Productivity enhancement comes in small ways as well as in the glamorous large cost reductions. It may be achieved by as simple an activity as examining existing administrative procedures. At Lane, we learned that production of the class schedule would require one more week than we had available. At a meeting on the project, it was discovered that preparation had included an expensive data processing step, the reason for which had been forgotten. Eliminating that step saved us a week in time plus some unnecessary computer expenditures.

Kendrick's suggestion that better health and safety plans promote productivity by reducing time lost to illness and accidents was affirmed on our campus.[12] Appointment of a manager to monitor and promote accident prevention has cut the number of accidents by a fourth, costs by not quite half, days lost by three-fourths, and insurance premiums by about half.

Without question, colleges and universities have a lot to learn about how best to apply productivity techniques to academe. To some degree, our efforts are like exploration: we cannot be sure precisely where we are going, precisely where we are in our quest, or

10. Arnold R. Deutsch, *The Human Resources Revolution: Communicate or Litigate* (New York: McGraw-Hill, 1979); and Merritt L. Kastens, *Redefining the Manager's Job: The Proactive Manager in a Reactive World* (New York: AMACOM, 1980).

11. *Managing*, pp. 41–42.

12. "Increasing Productivity," p. 196.

exactly what we have learned. But, we have to move toward productivity anyway. As Priest and Pickelman suggest, we have to discard "the notion that one needs to know all the answers (especially in measurement) before any gains or productivity increases can be realized."[13]

A willingness to take risks in the interest of potential gains in productivity is mandatory, as is the need to commit funds in the short range to save in the long range. For example, I put my neck on the block in urging the Lane board to spend $200,000 to implement our energy management program. It paid for itself in two years. But what if it hadn't? I would have been in position to identify with the car salesman who heard the potential customer protest the price of a compact car. "But, that's almost the cost of a big car," the customer said. "Well," said the salesman, "if you want economy, you've got to pay for it."

A productive management, Drucker says, means in large measure preparing today's colleges and universities for the future. Those institutions that lead tomorrow will do so in part because they have substantially higher productivity than average. That margin will give them the edge. Those of us who must lead today's efforts to get ready for tomorrow might heed John W. Gardner: "A society is continuously re-created, for good or ill, by its members. This will strike some as burdensome, but it will summon others to greatness."[14]

How to Endow an Air Conditioner: A Few Words to Presidents
Charles E. P. Simmons

The presidency of a college or university is no longer a genteel calling. Indeed, it is damned hard work, productive of a litany of woes. Today and into the 1990s, there is no precedent for what presidents must be prepared to do, explain, or "fund raise." Every-

13. *Increasing Productivity in the Community College*, p. 15.

14. *Self-Renewal: The Individual and the Innovative Society* (New York: Harper & Row, 1964), p. 137.

one gives presidents advice on the future, and most of it gets gloomier. Pundits and paragons vie to explain what we presidents can expect. As if the demographic picture were not bad enough, the economic picture increases the heartburn. Then add government regulations, Titles VI, VII, and IX—all in Roman numerals—and one can imagine oneself as Alice in Wonderland. Add energy and conservation to the puzzle of the presidency, and the result is the ninth level of Dante and I don't mean heaven.

Air conditioners are as important in saving money and energy as a football team was for Jack Oakie movies. But it was much more romantic to say we'd save the old Siwash team by putting on a production and raising the $1,000 needed. Imagine Dick Powell singing about the joys of "air conditioning." And yesterday's endowment theme was assumed to mean books, faculty salaries, and general excellence. How things change. Today, presidents' concerns are with development of facilities, government regulations, unionism, and energy.

Perhaps more distressing for education in the 1980s, we hear that out of five hundred presidents responding to a recent survey on their backgrounds, fewer than half had administrative training. Who would have thought presidents would deal with steam tunnels and heat and air conditioning surveys? Just where did all these experts come from who demand exorbitant fees to tell us where the thermostats should go? A president, when feeling particularly self-indulgent, could tell these latter-day entrepreneurs where they could go. Yet they serve to remind us that energy and maintenance are dominant issues. And foundations are taking a hard-line view that costs, productivity, and management are new conditions that need careful scrutiny. Indeed, in my case management extends to a very large equestrian center, and any president should count his or her blessings for not having my feed bill. (But then there is not much call for a Latin American historian, with emphasis on a seventeenth-century Mexican bishop. And let me hasten to wager that some other presidents' dissertations were equally useful.)

Unromantic and pedestrian as they may be, energy and maintenance on campus are areas where the public and private sector can agree with the King when he says to Anna, "Is a problem." In some instances, it can make or break an institution. Multipurpose institutions have a critical mass in their populations that permits greater flexibility and budget control. Smaller private liberal arts institutions have a clientele whose members pay increasingly higher tuition (which accounts for about 70 percent of the budget) and demand much more from resources and as outcomes of their educational costs. And the cacophony of trustees shouting to balance the budget is a continual nightmare.

Pity the president who allows the campus to look like the South Bronx. Students will not accept poor housing, and they are the consumers. Try allowing the grass to grow and windows to remain cracked, and your board will scream at the shoddy place. Of course we build energy and maintenance costs into the budget. What does that do for salaries and new programs? Windows—who would have thought ten years ago that at a meeting of the American Council on Education we would talk windows. On our campus at Lake Erie College we have a lovely commons building that won a design award in 1958. In the winter the building is cooler than the outside, and in the summer it is warmer. It is an all-glass rotunda, and windows take over center stage. Each frame costs $1,500 to replace, and in 1980 the bill came to $20,000. There are fifty-two large windows, and that does not count the "attractive" smaller ones. Try cleaning them! Suggestions to change the building are always forthcoming. One engineer suggested I board it up. Another, tear it down. But it did win a prize. Hock the prize and give me a building that is cost efficient.

When an entire campus is used for various activities during the summer, demands for service and cooling must be given a positive response. Summer school, conferences, and band, cheerleader, wrestling, and boxing camps create income. But have you ever faced a hot, belligerent football player sans air conditioning? Cost of the repair on the window seems small, but a $5 million budget, of which 52 percent goes for salaries and benefits, leaves little room for surprises and means a continual reassessing of priorities.

Taking Things in Hand

Imagination and a thick skin are needed, but presidential guidance is a must. There seems to be no lack of ideas on saving crankcase oil, say, in a major university system with a fleet of vehicles. And you may not have gas wells as Lake Erie College does, but Wells College's former president, Cissy Farenthold, came to our campus and said, "I am going to do that," and has. What one must be aware of is that inaction in energy conservation simply will not be accepted in the future by any board. Wells College is putting the money up front and could come up with a dry well. We leased the land, took an annual fee, and kept enough gas for our own emergency use. Another arrangement could be, if the board is "kicky," to have individual board members take the land, put their money into the drilling, and then deed the land back to the college.

After all, wasn't the Ph.D. awarded as recognition that you can analyze? Just because you do not have an "administrative" background is not a cause for worry. My greatest fear is the "manager." If we allow the green shades to take over, then higher education is in serious trouble. A colleague of mine has a famous business manager. But at the same time the FBM is a great cross. He has all the answers, has plans ready to redo the steam tunnels, the heat gauges, water lines, and lighting. And there's the rub: We *cannot* let the academic enterprise be decided by budget allocations made in a narrow sense. That marvelous commercial with Shakespeare saying he is endangered is truer than you think if we abrogate our educational expertise and leadership. But we must plan and set the priorities in the various energy and maintenance areas. So, along with academic planning, the energy plan must complement, not inhibit or destroy, the academic heart of the matter.

Trustees and legislators have to be educated about facts regarding college maintenance and conservation efforts. But the education must be based on facts, and not on emotional approaches. Basic assumptions must be spelled out with respect to average life of equipment, maintenance of vehicles, as well as why computer hardware must be replaced. In energy conservation measures, computers will increasingly be used. All these items must be fitted into a phased concept so that not everything comes due on one day. Cost of energy consumption by area and department must be worked out. No longer can you assign all water costs to one building, as we did to the theater center. When the bill for $60,000 in water rates came through at Lake Erie, it was a shock until the discovery was made that the old accounting system put all water bills in one building because that was easiest. No president will either impress boards or get a handle on costs with that approach. It will take us some time to get enough data to begin proper allocation of not only water costs but also, frankly, most of our other utility costs.

Let us then be leaders in energy conservation and see what can happen. As a member of the Energy Task Force of the American Council on Education, Association of Physical Plant Administrators, and the National Association of College and University Business Officers, I have become more aware that higher education does not respond well to this new crisis. We must provide, develop, and sustain energy management programs on campus. The list of items to be discussed and transmitted to the various colleges is horrendous: building energy performance, standards of lighting efficiency, renewable energy resources, studies of the federal energy conservation plan, solar energy, fuel, and the Natural Gas Act. Add to the list the technical assistance that will be needed for all campuses. The job of educating the various groups on campus is mind-boggling.

But, back to earth. The crisis is real; it will not go away. On my campus we need $60,000 for a new boiler.

Pieces of the Action

Can we offer some tentative solutions at least at the basic level of the problem in energy and maintenance?

Trustees perhaps are the easiest. The Association of Governing Boards of Universities and Colleges can deliver programs to help trustees see the problem. Again, however, some trustees look at education as a "business," and the bottom line mentality forgets we can charge our students only so much. Students will turn elsewhere if the costs continue to escalate and inflate. An energy surcharge, used at one institution, is a dangerous precedent, and rewards to students for turning off lights and water can lead to difficulties in balancing a budget. Boards must be prepared after consultation to lay out deferred maintenance and energy plans that do not affect in any way the academic program budget. And the board as a policy maker must demand that the president stick to the plan.

Faculty members must have some guidance because, except for those involved in research, they feel energy is not their responsibility. If they wish wage and benefit increases, then they've got to pay attention when the president begins planning the energy package. That package can be part of their benefits: air-conditioned offices for better research and teaching cost money. And the sooner they realize a hot library or a cold dorm can translate into lost students, the sooner they will respond. Although energy is not their primary responsibility, it nonetheless affects their primary task—teaching and having someone to teach.

Students should not be rewarded for saving energy; a little value development and an energy diet are important. Get the deans to work on a student energy plan: it will keep them busy. Put the best plan to work so that students find corporate responsibility and discipline rewarding, and you as president keep tuition costs down.

Alumnae need to be reminded when they say the grass needs mowing that giving is essential. We don't need sofas or honey pitchers in deferred-giving programs unless we can sell them for real dollars. Dusting such items increases college costs.

Finally, endow an air conditioner. Let all your clientele know what it costs to maintain and what it means in revenue. A practical point is bingo. We have bingo games in the gymnasium every Thursday, and the community groups have a good time. (And before that remark evokes derision, consider that New York University had a macaroni factory, Bloomfield a golf course, and one college a racetrack.) But people didn't come to the bingo games in the summer because it was simply too hot. Air conditioning upped the take, and scholarship money flowed again. And if you use the campus in summer, you need comfort. So I say endow air conditioning. It might lead to a trend. The J.R. Steam Tunnel and the Flo Thermostat.

Well, we have problems. But as Churchill said with Dunkirk behind him in the midst of the Battle of Britain, and as you should say, "I find it all quite exhilarating."

CIVILITY

Sexual Harassment and Women Students
Bernice Resnick Sandler

Sexual harassment is not really a new issue on campus. It has been hidden for years, with students suffering silently and alone. When Yale University was sued in 1977 under Title IX[1] by five students claiming sexual harassment by faculty, Pandora's box was opened: sexual harassment came out of the closet at last.

The focus here is on male harassment of female students, because in most academic settings, the majority of faculty and other staff are male. Although there are some instances of male students being propositioned by female professors or of a homosexual teacher harassing gay students, these are only a tiny fraction of sexual harassment incidents. Across the country, sexual harassment has increasingly become an issue of concern. Some examples will illustrate the scope.

At Harvard, a professor has received a formal reprimand. At the University of California, Berkeley, a professor was suspended for one quarter; and at San Jose State University, a tenured associate professor was fired when five students accused him of embracing, fondling, and propositioning them. At Arizona State University, the University of California, Berkeley, and the University of Minnesota, as well as other institutions, students are organizing such groups as the Coalition Against Sexual Harassment to deal with the issue. As other instances, at the University of Massachusetts at Boston, students are filing charges, and at Berkeley and the University of Rhode Island surveys are being conducted by students.

Still other activities may be cited. The American Psychological Association's Division of Psychology of Women has developed a task force to investigate the problem of sexual harassment. The National

Parts of this paper appeared in "Sexual Harassment: A Hidden Issue," prepared by the Project on the Status and Education of Women, 1978, which is included in the Sexual Harassment Packet (1818 R St., N.W., Washington, D.C. 20009: Association of American Colleges, the Project).

1. Title IX of the Education Amendments of 1972 prohibits sex discrimination in institutions receiving federal assistance.

Advisory Council on Women's Educational Programs has issued a report on sexual harassment of students in colleges and universities. And, further, such institutions as Stanford and Rutgers are beginning to develop policies and procedures to deal with sexual harassment.

The issue is difficult to deal with. For example, how to define sexual harassment is not easy. Certainly whenever men and women are together, sexual attraction and sexual relationships are a possibility. How to differentiate sexual harassment from ordinarily personal and private relationships is the crux of the problem in definition.

Sexual harassment covers a wide range of behaviors, from sexual innuendos made at inappropiate times, perhaps in the guise of humor, to coerced sexual relations. It may include
- verbal harassment or abuse such as insults, suggestive comments, and demands;
- subtle pressure for sexual activity;
- sexist remarks about a woman's clothing, body, or sexual activities;
- unnecessary touching, patting, or pinching;
- leering at or ogling a woman's body;
- demanding sexual favors accompanied by implied or overt threats concerning one's job, grades, letters of recommendation, and the like;
- physical assault—attempted or actual rape.

Although there may be instances of students who initiate or encourage sexual activities with male professors, harassment differs from ordinary or "acceptable" flirting, because in part it is *unwanted* and because it occurs in a power relationship where the parties are not equal. Moreover, in those instances where a woman has engaged in casual flirtation, she is likely to accept responsibility for the sexual advances that may follow; she is not likely to view or claim the consequences of her activity as sexual harassment. What characterizes the insidious nature of sexual harassment in academe is that the professor is in a position of authority.

Effects of Harassment on Students

A college professor wields considerable influence over a student's academic success and future career. A teacher's assessment of a student may quite directly affect her life's chances. Students depend on their professors for grades, recommendations, job referrals, and research-related opportunities. Graduate students, in addition, rely on their professors for opportunities to attend special seminars and conferences and to coauthor research papers, for introductions to colleagues in the field, for sponsorship in informal and formal academic societies and professional associations, and for recommendations for grants, fellowships, and faculty appointments. The woman graduate student's working relationship with a faculty member is developed on a one-to-one basis within small seminars, research projects, independent study, and tutorials. The professor serves as an academic advisor and is a key figure in her academic progress. As the job market tightens and competition for employment opportunities intensifies, faculty influence increases.

When sexual harassment occurs, it creates a chilling effect on the learning climate. To refuse sexual demands may mean the woman is jeopardizing her academic career. A woman cannot freely choose to say yes or no in such a situation. The student fears retaliation and often with good reason: Rejected males do not always respond with good grace. Reprisals are not unusual. Unfair grades may be given. The student may be fearful of any interaction with the professor: How can she ask for an appointment for advice on her work if she is worried that the professor is likely to touch her or ask for sexual favors? Students have dropped courses, changed their majors, transferred to another school, or even discontinued their education in response to harassment.

Scope and Characteristics

Like rape, sexual harassment has been a hidden problem, treated as a joke or blamed on the victim herself. A long history of silence on the subject has made many women feel uncomfortable, embarrassed, or ashamed. They are afraid that any mention will reflect badly on their own character or that somehow they will be viewed as having invited the behavior. Often, they do blame themselves, just as women in many situations blame themselves for the actions of others. They may feel unjustified guilt and be fearful of repercussions. They may even feel too ashamed to tell friends, husband, or family.

The student who is harassed is in a double bind. She may be unsure whether a real injustice has occurred. If she ignores the situation, it rarely goes away. If she takes a strong stand, the professor may retaliate. He may deny it; he may make light of it and tell her she's not a good sport. He may pretend that she initiated the encounter, or that she's flattering herself by imagining she was being propositioned. If she complains elsewhere, she may be ignored, be told she ought to be able to handle it herself, or be labeled as a troublemaker.

Furthermore, if sexual harassment remains a hidden issue, students may find that simple friendliness or academic enthusiasm may be misinterpreted by faculty members as a sexual invitation. Yet, if they avoid friendliness with male professors, they may not receve intellectual support, grants, and the important mentoring that is essential for professional growth.

How widespread is sexual harassment of students? The absence of complaints does not mean the absence of the problem. In a study at the University of California, Berkeley, 30 percent of female seniors stated that they were harassed by at least one professor at Berkeley or at another college.[2] A study by the National Advisory Council on Women's Educational Programs uncovered over 160 instances of sexual harassment.[3] In the work place, estimates range as high as 92 percent.[4] (A recent study of federal employees found that 42 percent of women had suffered unwanted sexual advances on the job.[5]) Moreover, sexual harassment affects a wide range of students and older reentry women. Nor is harassment limited to professors only; other staff members such as counselors and health service personnel may also be involved.

The question of teacher-student sex is a delicate matter. Certainly not all women students experience harassment nor do most professors proposition their students. Some students and faculty do not regard sexual harassment as a problem. Others may not believe it exists. Some are quick to point to the apparently seductive behavior of some women students.

Some college and university administrators feel that whether teacher-student sexual relations occur, it's nobody's business. Yet to the person who feels coerced into such a relationship, the problem

2. Donna Benson, "The Sexualization of Student-Teacher Relationships" (2829 Forest Ave., Berkeley, Calif. 94705).

3. An analysis of institutional liability appears in *Sexual Harassment: A Report on the Sexual Harassment of Students* (1832 M St., N.W., Washington, D.C. 20036: National Advisory Council on Women's Educational Programs, 1980).

4. See, for example, Lin Farley, *Sexual Shakedown* (New York: McGraw-Hill, 1978); Catherine McKinnon, *Sexual Harassment of Working Women* (New Haven, Conn.: Yale University Press, 1979); Letty Cottin Pogrebin, "The Working Woman: Sex Harassment," *Ladies Home Journal*, June 1977; and *Sexual Harassment at the Workplace* (Box 1, Cambridge, Mass. 02139: Alliance Against Sexual Coercion).

5. Obtain information about the study from Merit Systems Protection Board, Washington, D.C. 20419.

may be overwhelming, especially since few universities have a *formal* channel through which she may complain. Given both the desire to do well in one's academic field and the seriousness of the charge of sexual harassment, most women find themselves in an untenable position.

Sexual harassment is not, of course, solely a women's issue. Both men and women—students and faculty—suffer under a system that fails to provide established remedies. An indirect result of sexual harassment on campus is that some male faculty members may be so cautious or concerned about the possible implications of a friendship with their female students that many women are shut out from the friend-teacher relationships that provide an invaluable learning experience for male students. The result is that female students are afforded more limited academic opportunity than their male peers and fewer opportunities to obtain good job recommendations. It appears that whether women are confronted with sexual propositions or are left alone because of the potential for harassment, women students are inhibited in their pursuit of educational and professional goals.

Legal Implications

Does Title IX prohibit sexual harassment of students? Apparently yes.[6] The Yale law suit opened that door, although the student lost the case for failing to prove that an improper advance was made or that she was adversely affected as a consequence. The Department of Education considers sexual harassment as a violation of Title IX and has sent out several letters of findings confirming this view.

Under Title IX, institutions are required to have a grievance procedure to deal with problems of sex discrimination. Thus, institutions are required to have a procedure to deal with sexual harassment complaints. (The procedure does not have to be the same as that which handles other discrimination complaints.) Institutions are likely to be liable under Title IX when (1) the harasser was an employee or agent of the institution; (2) the harasser was in a position to affect the academic success of the victim, through grades, recommendations, and the like, or the climate for learning was negatively

6. The National Advisory Council has issued a legal memorandum, "Sexual Harassment: Fact of Life or Violation of Law? University Liability Under Title IX" (July 1, 1978), written by Alexandra Polyzoides Buck, an attorney formerly with the General Counsel's office, U.S. Department of Health, Education, and Welfare. The paper concludes that Title IX does prohibit sexual harassment.

affected or both; (3) the harassment involved only members of one sex; (4) the institutions did not provide prompt remedies or corrective action once it knew or should have known that incidences of sexual harassment had occurred.

The report by The National Advisory Council on Women's Educational Programs also suggests that institutions might be liable in some instances when students sexually harass other students, particularly when the act or acts interfere with the learning climate and the institution did not provide relief once it knew or should have known that acts of sexual harassment had taken place.[7] An example might be a professor who encourages or allows male students to make abusive sexual remarks in class.

State laws may also cover sexual harassment. Students may be able to claim tort damage or civil wrongs and thus sue the institution or the harasser or both for monetary relief. Students might also be able to bring criminal action in cases of sexual crimes such as assault or sexual abuse. Additionally, institutions are required under Title IX to publish a notice that they do not discriminate. That notice might be construed as creating a contractual obligation between students and the institution, so that a student who did not obtain relief when she complained of sexual harassment might sue for breach of contract; that is, the institution promised a nondiscriminatory climate and failed to do so when it did not prevent sexual harassment.

Still other possibilities—all untried as yet—exist. Could an institution be sued for "aiding and abetting" if it did nothing in a situation where criminal laws applied? Could a faculty member be charged with assault and battery? (In Massachusetts a dentist was fined $1,000 for kissing a patient without warning.) Are rape laws, as well as assault with intent to rape, applicable? How pertinent are sexual abuse laws? (In New York a man who pinched a woman's backside in the subway was convicted when a judge ruled that "buttocks are an intimate part of a person" and therefore covered by the state's sexual abuse law.)

What the Institution Can Do

Fortunately institutions can do more than merely wait for charges of sexual harassment to be brought. Although the suggestions listed may not be appropriate for every institution, they are likely to be helpful in alleviating the situation.

7. National Advisory Council, *Sexual Harassment.*

- *Develop a policy prohibiting sexual harassment.* Having a formal policy in place is likely to prevent many instances of sexual harassment.
- *Disseminate the policy to faculty, staff, and students.*
- *Develop a procedure to inform new staff, new faculty members, and new students about the policy.*
- *Develop a grievance procedure to handle complaints.* The procedure need not be identical to other grievance mechanisms if not appropriate. Institutions might find a two-step procedure helpful: a mechanism to resolve complaints informally, followed by a formal procedure if the first procedure has been unsuccessful. Although students cannot be required to use a grievance procedure, and can indeed bypass it by filing a complaint with the U.S. Department of Education, they are less likely to do so or to go to court if the institution has a procedure for them to use.
- *Disseminate information about the grievance procedure* to faculty members, students, and staff.
- *Develop pamphlets advising women students* about their rights as well as how to handle and, where possible, avoid sexual harassment. Such a pamphlet could be developed by a campus committee on the status of women or a women's center. The provost's office at Michigan State University and the Committee on the Status of Women at Utah State University have developed materials that tell students steps they can take, and lists university groups and persons who can be asked for help.
- *Develop pamphlets for men college students, staff, and faculty members* about the nature of sexual harassment and its legal implications.
- *Document the problem* by surveys, hearings, meetings, or other means. Sponsor a campuswide conference or speak-out organized by students, staff, and faculty members to sensitize the academic community to the issue of sexual harassment. Bringing sexual harassment into the public arena will build support for institutional policies and procedures.
- *Develop a faculty code of conduct.*
- *Include materials on sexual harassment in courses on human sexuality.*
- *Include materials on sexual harassment in student handbooks.*
- *Train counselors and other student personnel* to deal with sexual harassment issues raised by students.
- *Establish a twenty-four-hour crisis hotline* to provide counseling

and referral services to students concerned with the problem of sexual harassment. The hotline could be sponsored by a campus counseling center or a women's group.

Additionally, research is needed to analyze the causes and extent of, and remedies for, sexual harassment on campus. The problem of sexual harassment will not go away, nor are there easy answers. The issues are complex and not readily resolved. The problem can no longer be hidden. And institutions must move forward, not because of legal requirements, but because they care about the educational climate of their students.

Civility on Campus—Pressures to Ameliorate Intergroup Conflict

Theodore Freedman

During the 1979–80 academic year, college campuses experienced a rash of incidents of varying intensity, ranging from name calling to desecrations to vandalism to physical violence. The Anti-Defamation League (ADL), with which I am associated, recently looked at these incidents critically to determine whether they were simply aberrations or were symptomatic of a more serious problem on campuses.

ADL viewed these events with special concern because their location and scope carried ominous overtones. Ideally, the campus has been viewed as society's important bastion of education and enlightenment. Charles Y. Glock, formerly of the University of California, Berkeley, and chief sociologist of the monumental study series "Patterns of American Prejudice" (in which the ADL participated), cited the level of education, more than income or occupation, as the key to an individual's propensity to prejudice.[1] In fact, *all* research clearly indicates that prejudice decreases as the level of education increases. Thus, bigotry in our institutions of higher learning should be expected to be nonexistent.

That desirable situation does not appear to be the case, based on ADL's initial data. We surveyed ninety colleges and universities

1. New York: Harper & Row.

through questionnaires sent to specifically identifiable and presumably knowledgeable persons in four sectors (Hillel directors, heads of student government, editors of campus newspapers, and deans of students) at each institution. To date we have received 150 responses representing eighty of the institutions surveyed. Of the institutions, 41 percent (thirty-three institutions) reported experiencing some kind of incident or incidents during the past year.

Incidents

Without belaboring all the data, three illustrations from broad categories will suffice: 14 percent of the reported incidents were related to fraternities, athletes, and athletics events; 24 percent could be generally described as some form of vandalism; and 28 percent were political in nature, such as anti-Israel, anti-Zionist, anti-black and Third World, or Klan related.

Vandalism. Such incidents included the destruction of property belonging to Jewish fraternities and the prolific use of Nazi symbols and epithets. Related but somewhat different in form is the second category.

Fraternities and athletics. At Babson College (Massachusetts), anti-Semitism was used to get the team "up" for a soccer match with Brandeis University. A sign in the dining room proclaimed "Happy Holocaust." At another soccer match between North Adams State College (Massachusetts) and Brandeis, team members verbally abused their opponents with anti-Semitic slurs. After a complaint was registered with officials and one North Adams player was ejected from the game, anti-Semitic shouting erupted from the stands, which finally necessitated a plea over the loudspeaker that the insulting remarks end. At the University of Miami (Florida), a Jewish campus worker walking at night on the campus was physically abused and thrown into a lake by members of the football team. Similar incidents involving fraternities were reported at the University of Florida and the University of Georgia.

The political level. At Ithaca College (New York), eleven white students paraded around the campus as Ku Klux Klansmen with other students portraying blacks being taken as slaves. There was a reaction, and violence was narrowly averted. Black students lodged a complaint citing "mental abuse and inciting others to violate the college's code." Seven of the eleven students were suspended for the year, and the suspended students have appealed the action of the administration in the state supreme court. It is particularly noteworthy that the campus community is reportedly split on whether the severity of the punishment was appropriate. Little discussion has gone to the meaning or implications of the incident itself. At the University of Pittsburgh, students identified as members of the Palestine Solidarity Committee and the Anti-Imperialist Union harassed and physically abused a group displaying pro-Israel materials, to the point that the police had to be called to subdue the attackers.

The Potential for Increased Conflict

Now, and certainly within the last ten years, more than at any time in the history of higher education, the student body stands as a microcosm of American society, with a similar diversity of views and action. Accordingly, as a nation, we are, perhaps more than we care to admit, a splintered America. The 1980 political campaign dramatically revealed the intensity of single issue politics. Further, we have embraced cultural pluralism (positively, I admit) not only to reassert ancestral languages and cultures, but also to recognize a demand for a particular group's civil rights. We appear to have done so, unmindful of the needs of other groups and of the possible divisive effects of such recognition. We have, in my judgment, gone so far in fostering ethnicity that we have failed to accompany this legitimate drive with a concomitant view of the common good. Rather than seeing America as a mosaic of cooperating cultures, differing in life styles within American democracy and nationhood, we may run the risk of developing a separatism akin to that of many French-speaking Canadians in Quebec Province. And still further, we are witnessing increased recruiting activities by the Ku Klux Klan on or near school campuses and at some high schools as well.

Also to be considered is the potential for importing to the United States and to the campus acts of terrorism prevalent in the Middle East, Europe, and Latin America. Those caught up in a "theology of liberation" appear to support any means to achieve a so-called just political objective.

On October 3, 1980, the *San Francisco Chronicle* reported an incident in which an Iranian national planned to bomb a meeting of supporters of the Ayatollah Khomeini at San Jose State University. The student, described as a member of the Iranian Free Army, planned to detonate two pipe bombs at a meeting where students were to discuss peace efforts in the Middle East. Although the next example is not campus-related, little imagination is needed to transfer it to the campus. A report in the *San Francisco Chronicle* of October 10, 1980, describes the pipe bombing of the San Francisco women's building that houses thirteen women's groups including, among others, the National Organization for Women. Stanford Lyman, a sociologist at the New School for Social Research, who was attending the National Conference on Chinese American Studies, stated that "it is a myth in America that race relations are a temporary problem that will one day go away. There will always be race relations. The question is what kind will they be: friendly and intimate, or hostile and distrustful?"

The Responsibility to Respond Creatively to Conflict

Let me return to the situation at Ithaca College. The action of that administration was, in my view, forthright and proper in its tone. The attitude of the students is more problematic. They focused solely on the suspensions and not the larger issues and apparently were given no help or guidance in their thinking.

The ADL's overall findings indicate that administrators reflect uncertainty, if not confusion, about an appropriate response to these kinds of incidents. They demonstrate a tendency to down-play the severity of incidents and to characterize them as isolated acts of misfits. More specifically, administrators are reluctant to deal with matters that might lead to accusations of limiting free speech.

Administrators, faculty members, and staff can well keep in mind a few suggestions to aid them in their efforts.
- Administrators should make it unequivocally clear that they oppose such behavior and will do all within their power to deal with such conflicts in a forthright manner.
- Administrators should convene a meeting of fraternity and sorority leaders to encourage and help them to develop programs within their own groups to sensitize and educate their members about intergroup conflict and its resolution.
- The same kind of approach should be used with representatives of the student council, to work within the existing campus organizations and to discuss broad campus programs as well.
- Perhaps most difficult, administrators should meet with department chairpersons, especially those teaching history, sociology, psychology, government, and the like, to explore how, in a classroom, an ugly, dangerous, and damaging incident can become a carefully structured and meaningful learning experience.

INTERNATIONALIZING CURRICULA

Internationalizing the Community College Curriculum

Moses S. Koch

In 1973, Alan Pifer, then president of the Carnegie Corporation of New York, spoke to the annual meeting of the American Association of Community and Junior Colleges. He emphasized an expanding role for community colleges, not as the junior partners in higher education, but as institutional agents of societal change. Among the changes that are engaging attention from some community colleges is "internationalizing" the curriculum. Two related definitions will help guide the discussion.

1. *International education* can be any one or a combination of deliberately designed learning activities, such as study abroad, foreign language studies or area studies, faculty and student exchange programs, technical assistance in other countries, interdisciplinary emphasis on international studies, and so on. Always, the goal is the development of attitudes, knowledge, and behavior with respect to matters international and global.

2. An *internationalized curriculum* is an ultimate vehicle toward which all efforts in international education contribute. A semester overseas, faculty and student exchange programs, courses in languages and in area studies, and various other efforts in international education contribute toward internationalizing the curriculum.

For a two-year college to internationalize its curriculum effectively, every graduating student should have gained some substantial experience with respect to international and intercultural affairs as part of the college's educational and developmental efforts. Thus, the internationalized curriculum should represent an institutional value commitment, a thematic, collegewide thrust to which all degree students are exposed. Allan Ostar, president of the American Association of State Colleges and Universities, has the view that "to be successful, an international curriculum must be university-wide. . . . The successful program is not really a program, but a strategy to infuse the entire university curriculum with an international dimension."[1]

Ostar's emphasis on infusion and Pifer's view of community colleges as agents of societal change mandate a reexamination of the two-year college curriculum—a process that is becoming widespread in the nation's colleges. For a major example, at Harvard University, Dean Henry Rosovsky, in a proposal to the Faculty of Arts and Sciences, cited five statements of rationale for changing Harvard's undergraduate curriculum. One of the statements refers to international education.

> An educated American in the last third of this century, cannot be . . . ignorant of other cultures. . . . It is no longer possible to conduct our lives without reference to the wider world within which we live. A crucial difference between the educated and the uneducated is the extent to which one's life experience is viewed in wider contexts.
> . . . The intention here is . . . to expose students to the essential and distinctive features of major alien cultures, whether Western or non-Western.[2]

Thus the report distributed to Harvard's faculty declares that a major element in meeting the requirements of the late twentieth century is international education. It places "foreign languages and cultures" on an equal plane of importance with requirements in literature and the arts, history, social and philosophical analysis, and sciences and mathematics.

In Support of Internationalizing the Curriculum

Essentially four basic elements constitute the rationale for internationalizing the curriculum.

1. The fundamental, though not necessarily most acceptable, rationale may be termed the "blue marble" reason. Willis H. Griffin, a leading philosopher in international education, uses the image: "Pictures of the earth as a 'blue marble,' sent back by the astronauts . . . help to re-establish the unity of mankind and the oneness of the earth."[3] This global village view stresses the commonality of

1. Ostar, "The Global World of Work: Are We Preparing Students Adequately for International Careers?" *Bulletin of the Association of Departments of Foreign Languages*, May 1977, p. 14.

2. "Report on the Core Curriculum," Harvard University, February 15, 1978, p. 4.

3. Griffin, "International Educational Cooperation and the World's Future," *Topics in Cultural Learning*, vol. 3 (Honolulu: East-West Center, East-West Cultural Learning Institute, 1975), p. 137.

needs and desires of all cultures and people in our technologically compressed planet.

Robert S. McNamara, former U.S. Secretary of Defense and later president of the World Bank, has described some probable ramifications for our nation.

> [T]he trend toward increasing interdependence will shape our future in ways that we are just beginning to understand. Few among us realize that food shortages in sub-Saharan States will cause bread prices to rise in the supermarkets and will lead to wage increases in the auto industry. Even less are we aware that within our lifetime population growth in Mexico is very likely to cause the Spanish-speaking population in this country to multiply severalfold and to become the largest minority group in the nation, with all that implies for social stress and institutional change.[4]

Farmers, miners, production line workers—all feel the effects that developments in other countries have for this country in, say, prices, wages, and unemployment. Every community in the United States is a part of the world picture and therefore every citizen needs a world view. Our crowded planet is a mandate for a reorientation of persons, individually and collectively. In his Nobel Laureate address, Alexander Solzhenitsyn stated, "All internal affairs have ceased to exist on our crowded earth. The salvation of mankind lies only in making everything the concern of all."

2. The second rationale is a spinoff of the first. There is only one economy on this planet now—a world economy. Peter Drucker, economist and management theoretician, makes the cold analysis: "There is no 'sovereignty' anymore in an interdependent world economy. The emergence of trans-national bank-managed money is a . . . consequence . . . of the economic integration of the world economy." His main point is that "an integrated world economy in a world . . . splintered [politically] can co-exist only in tension, conflict and mutual misunderstanding."[5] Thus, if we believe in reducing tension and conflict, though not necessarily reducing differences, in our economically interdependent world, we must educate for that goal because little education has realistically been so directed.

Burns Weston, law professor at the University of Iowa, puts the issue boldly: "enlightened self-interest requires societies everywhere

---

4. McNamara, interviewed by Leonard Silk, *New York Times*, April 2, 1978.

5. *Managing in Turbulent Times* (New York: Harper & Row, 1980), pp. 109, 167, 170.

to begin *now*, if it is not already too late, to educate people in earnest both about the constraints and opportunities of global peril and about the burdens and benefits of global change."[6]

3. The ethical imperative rationale for internationalizing the curriculum responds to expectations of some of the developing countries. It calls for a reassessment of international ethics, partially through education. The Belgrade charter recognized this necessity by declaring

> We need nothing short of a new global ethic, [a]n ethic which
> . . . recognizes and sensitively responds to the complex and ever-
> changing relationships between man and nature, and between man
> and man. . . . Before this . . . can be achieved millions of individ-
> uals will themselves need to . . . assume a "personal and individual-
> ized global ethic." . . . The reform of educational . . . systems is
> central to the building of this new . . . ethic.[7]

4. The pragmatic rationale relates to mobility. The proportion of Americans traveling abroad and working abroad continues to grow, as does the number of non-Americans in the United States. It is appropriate that public education should provide U.S. citizens some preparation for this likely experience and for leadership in inter-national affairs. The community college, as an educational agency serving all adult ages as well as college-age persons, is a natural to fulfill this need.

Why the Community College?

Many community colleges will encounter internal and external resistance to internationalizing their curricula. They must therefore assemble the best responses possible to the question, Why is inter-national education the appropriate concern of community colleges? Aware of the rationales cited above, a critic may justly ask, "These reasons apply to Harvard University and to other four-year under-graduate curricula, but why should the two-year college feel particu-larly well qualified to extend its offerings into international educa-tion? By its very designation as a *community* college, the American two-year college should focus on the community, not on the world." This challenge has been answered by Edmund Gleazer, formerly

6. "Contending with a Planet in Peril: An Optimal Educational Response," *Alternatives, A Journal of World Policy*, June 1979, pp. 59–95. (Center for the Study of Developing Societies, Institute for World Order.)

7. "The Belgrade Charter, Framework for Environmental Education," *Nature Study*, vol 29. nos. 3–4, pp. 6–7.

president of the American Association of Community and Junior Colleges:

> First . . . is . . . the large numbers of people contacted. More than half of all students beginning their college work do so in community colleges. . . .
>
> Community colleges have fast become one of the nation's major resources in adult education. . . . If the institutions were to develop international dimensions, the numbers of people affected could be larger than those served by another segment of post-secondary education.
>
> Another asset of the community college in furthering its services is the network of relationships it has established in concert with other "educational providers" in the community . . . with community schools, public libraries, newspapers, radio and television stations, university extensions, museums, art galleries, departments of parks and recreation, labor unions, and training directors in business and industries. A reorientation of the community college to global dimensions and international collaboration will find its expression broadly extended by means of networks already in place.[8]

Models of Programs in International Education

The relationships Gleazer refers to offer a range of program possibilities—some models existing, some proposed. Among the two-year colleges, Rockland Community College in New York State and Brevard Community College in Florida have become active in foreign travel and education overseas. Miami-Dade Community College leads the two-year colleges in the enrollment of foreign students. Several community colleges have offered technical assistance to foreign institutions and countries. West Valley Community College in California offers summer international work experience for its students. These efforts at international exposure supposedly could indicate that all faculty and at least most students at the colleges are aware of the international education mission. However, most college students can graduate without any deliberate exposure to international or transnational matters—beyond possibly a course in European history or the like.

---

8. "International Dimensions and Community College Education, or Adapting to the Realities of a Changing Planet" (Paper delivered at the National Conference of the Community College Cooperative for International Development, on post-secondary education in the international community, Disney World, Florida, February 2, 1978).

Monroe Community College in New York State, aided by a federal grant, is attempting to introduce cross-cultural, international, and global components as modules into courses that are already required or popular or both, as part of a long-range plan toward internationalizing the college's curriculum. Monroe, in another significant effort in international education, is cooperating with the University of Zagreb and the State University of New York. The college has held the first two-year college conference between any socialist and nonsocialist countries. From October 26 to November 5, 1980, a delegation of twelve Yugoslav two-year college educators met with counterparts in New York State, in the first of two conferences, and the second took place in Yugoslavia in May 1981. The stated aims were to improve understanding between the two-year colleges of the two countries; from that mutual understanding, to learn from each other and thus improve their institutions; and to arrange for faculty and student exchanges.

Other strategies and offerings found in two-year and four-year colleges include modern language requirements; language and area studies; interdisciplinary studies of world problems such as population, resources, and peace; a semester or summer abroad; academic credit for foreign travel; student exchange; and faculty exchange.

Proposals for international standardization of the curriculum range as far as a recommendation for

> an international standardization of the curriculum and thus also for an international standardization of the examination requirements and qualifications. . . . [This] international cooperation has the advantage that through it many of those national ways of thinking, traditions and taboos obstructing . . . development can be overcome more easily.[9]

This statement was made by Gustav Thuro, leader of a German-Yugoslav group known as the Initiative Group, which is interested in improving and internationalizing the quality of instruction in higher education. The statement is an extreme in the range of proposals to internationalize education and may represent a conflict American educators will face as they attempt to interrelate with traditional foreign systems by internationalizing through standardization.

---

9. "Skeleton Strategy of the Development of a Level System of Polyvalent Curricula for the Entire Educational System" (Paper, Fachhochschule, Hamburg, January 1977).

In 1979, a special commission appointed by President Carter reported on its charge to examine the condition of international education and the study of foreign languages in the United States. The commission recommended sweeping reforms at all levels of American education to increase international understanding and to increase the language capabilities of Americans.

Griffin refers to a number of promising initiatives:

The World Council for Curriculum and Instruction . . .is . . . dealing with education for peace, a world based curriculum, and learning for global survival.

The World Order Models Project, sponsored by the Institute for World Order, involves academics and others from eight different parts of the world in formulating proposals for the structure of global relations in the decades ahead.

The Institute for World Order . . . is devoted to building a world order of peace, social justice, economic well-being, and ecological balance. . . . Through a broad program of education and policy research, the Institute engages a global network of students, educators, and scholars, as well as social critics, policy leaders, and activists in helping to bring about a more just world order.

Universities and the Quest for Peace, an organization with university membership around the world, is establishing in Geneva a transnational studies center committed to the promotion of education free from national bias.

The Consortium on Peace Research, Education and Development (COPRED), presently headquartered at Bethel College . . . [in] Kansas, is a membership organization devoted to networking, catalyzing, and serving persons and institutions interested in scientific study, actions/research, and education on problems of peace and social justice. It maintains association with UNESCO and the Finland based International Peace Research Association. . . .

United States federal legislation has spurred experimentation with interdisciplinary programs in a few colleges and universities aimed at providing an international dimension to general education and teacher education programs.

The creation of the United Nations University is of obvious significance.

The International Mankind Project of the Council for the Study of Mankind [brought] together educators from several countries in cooperative effort to reorder elementary school curricula and to develop teaching materials which focus on mankind concepts. . . . [The] educators [were] from Israel, Thailand, Sweden, India, Ghana, and the United States.

[The] World Council for Curriculum and Instruction . . . involves the teacher training branches of four universities in four countries: The University of Keele in England, the University of

Ibadan in Nigeria, the University of Malaysia, and Indiana University. . . . The aims of this project are to develop cooperatively a rationale and theoretical structure for world studies, and to produce and try out curricula materials for use both in teacher education programs and in schools.[10]

Recommendations

Several significant activities currently *within reach* can facilitate internationalizing our curricula. Following are some examples.

More integrated planning. Most of the efforts toward internationalizing the curriculum have been developed independently rather than as part of an institutionwide plan. Even our consortia cooperate on a scale limited mostly to study and travel abroad. It is time for two-year colleges to examine their international thrusts and to formulate integrated plans, including evaluative measures. They should not continue to depend on ad hoc, fragmentary efforts of a few dedicated persons. I believe the Yugoslav–U.S. Conference of Two-Year Colleges, noted above, can contribute to this objective.

Capitalizing on vacations abroad. Every year, particularly in summer, many cost-free opportunities are available to build bridges of international education—trips abroad by faculty members, administrators, and students. Few of these travelers attempt to develop contacts with their counterparts in the host country. A "busman's holiday"—informal scheduled conferences with counterparts abroad—is an easy, inexpensive way to elicit active participation by educators, students, and community leaders in international education. Sister Cities Programs are an example.

Massive Canadian and Mexican exchanges with the United States. Colleges and universities in our country should consider undertaking massive student and faculty exchange programs with Canada and Mexico, as a model for adaptation beyond those two countries. In so doing, consideration should be given to methods of reducing the costs to students.

Improvement of communication between higher education and the United Nations. American higher education needs to develop ways for its professionals in higher education to learn about what is going on in other nations and in the United Nations. Thus we may hope to evolve a link between American higher education policy and world affairs.

10. Griffin, "International Education Cooperation," p. 137.

Appropriate as a conclusion is a statement approved by the membership of the American Association of State Colleges and Universities in 1975:

> The globalization of education should not be on the fringes of the curriculum, "the frosting on the cake." Rather, it must be institutionalized as an integral part of the pedagogical philosophy of the institution and its curriculum. *There is no student presently in college who should be exempted from acquiring some sensitivity to the existence, diversity, and dynamic inter-relationship of the many cultures in our world society.*[11] [italics added]

Foreign Students and Institutional Policy—Who's in Charge?
John F. Reichard

For the academic year 1980–81, *Open Doors*, the Institute of International Education's annual census of foreign students and scholars enrolled in U.S. colleges and universities, will, for the first time, report the figure at 300,000—a growth of nearly 30,000 in one year.[1] For part of that year, relations between the leading sender of students, Iran, and the United States underwent such extraordinary convulsions that it seemed the figure of 50,000 Iranian students would decline markedly. Through the entire incredible experience of the hostage crisis, the Immigration and Naturalization Service reported that no more than 5,000 Iranian students left voluntarily or through deportation.

Meanwhile the renewal of exchange relations with the People's Republic of China stimulated in just two years a large flow to the United States, as reported by the U.S.–China Education Clearinghouse, organized jointly by the National Academy of Sciences and the National Association for Foreign Student Affairs (NAFSA).

11. Ostar, "The Global World of Work," p. 13.

1. The annual census is conducted with program assistance from the American Association of Collegiate Registrars and Admissions Officers and the National Association for Foreign Student Affairs.

Six thousand Chinese now study here. The newly industrialized nations of Asia have contributed significantly to the growth in foreign student enrollments, as have Third World Commonwealth countries, whose students now face "full cost" fees in the United Kingdom. And as tourists from developed nations have discovered, the floating value of the dollar internationally has made the purchase of U.S. services—even inflation-prone U.S. higher education—more accessible. Meanwhile the new pied pipers of U.S. higher education—the overseas recruiters—are playing their songs quite effectively to students in the oil-rich countries.

All of these flows led a University of Colorado economist to suggest to the American Economic Association that three-quarters of a million students was not an unreasonable expectation by 1990 if colleges and universities fully exploit the worldwide interest in those applied fields—technology and business—in which U.S. higher education has unusual educational capabilities. Other educators have said a million students from abroad is not out of the question.

The State of Affairs

Something happened, however, on the way to the one million foreign student market. In a word, "Iran." The national trauma over the fifty-two hostages brought into clear focus several matters that had deserved close attention from various communities. The list makes a litany of bumblings: the disorderly growth of the Iranian student population in our country, and the failure to balance that population properly; inattention to the movement of Iranians into internationally inexperienced and administratively unprepared colleges and into certain aggressive proprietary institutions (and the rapid movement out by many dissatisfied and confused Iranians); the apparent failure of relatively large international educational and cultural interchange programs to produce understanding between the United States and Iran; the conspicuous political demonstrations of fanatical students who Americans thought (and still think) "should go home if they don't like it here"; the virtual bureaucratic shambles of the Immigration and Naturalization Service, which, when called upon to say how many Iranians were in the United States, could not reply to the Attorney General and then, when ordered to find out, undertook a massive assault on the integrity of international education, through a series of unseemly crackdowns on the Iranians,

202 INTERNATIONALIZING CURRICULA

followed by a proposal (now abandoned) for U.S. registration of all foreign students.

Meanwhile state legislatures were dashing forth to tilt Iranian windmills as well. Attempts to restrict Iranian student registrations failed on a number of campuses and also in state capitols across the Sunbelt (and Massachusetts, Illinois, and New Jersey legislative bodies, too, heard anti-foreign student cries). More seriously, some state legislators for the first time became aware of foreign students and began to study how to take action against them. Since no one in higher education had ever thought to explain to state legislators (with a few exceptions such as Minnesota and Michigan) the purposes and values of international education, it was not surprising that a wave of righteous indignation would overcome lawmakers—especially in an election year. It is too soon to say what effect the collision of recruiting scandals and of demonstrating Iranian students will have on the ardor of some colleges and universities to fill classrooms and the drive of vast overseas student populations to move toward the lodestone of the American degree. However, the time has come to take a thoughtful look at foreign students—who they are, why they came here, what their presence means to U.S. higher education, who is paying for the interchange, what their special needs are, who is benefiting from the experience. In short, what are the costs and values of international education as engaged in by U.S. colleges and universities? Who is in charge of this growing process? Who, if anyone, should be?

At the 1979 Conference on International Education, in an address titled, "Global Context: the U.S. Role," Ohio State's Harold L. Enarson commented:

> Most of us believe that it's good to have foreign students on campus, good for faculty to enjoy Fulbrights, good for faculty to take overseas assignments with Brazil or the World Bank or UNESCO or the Sudanese Department of Agriculture.
>
> Most of us believe that it's good to take a foreign student to Rotary Club. It shows how cosmopolitan we are. This symbolic gesture saves us the burden of asking what the other 999 or 1,999 foreign students are experiencing in the community.
>
> Most of us believe it's good to have some sort of an international club on campus for foreign students. It shows we care. So perhaps once or twice a year we have "international day" and enjoy Taiwanese cooking and Brazilian guitar. That symbolic gesture saves us the burden of asking what foreign students are experiencing in the dorms and in their classes and in their lives.

More than Good Intentions

American institutions of higher education are exceptionally diverse, with a history of independence in their development and with the freedom and resources to design innovative educational curricula to meet the needs of a rapidly growing and changing society. The country's international exchange activities have reflected that diversity, freedom, resourcefulness, and inventiveness. As a partial result, the Fulbright and many nongovernmental undertakings have had exceptional excellence. The trouble is that *sponsored* programs, such as the Fulbright, are far too few, and their numbers and stipends have been in serious decline for a decade while unsponsored exchanges grew enormously. Many serious scholars can no longer afford the Fulbright honor so that the search for qualified applicants is urgent, even in prestigious programs. The American Council on Education's Board of Directors recognized the seriousness of the situation in a special resolution on scholarly exchanges in early 1980:

> Of all the international communications media at our disposal, scholarly exchange ranks among the highest in its long-range, permeative effect. In times of peculiar international tension, however, its benefits can recede in the national consciousness, and its public policy support can be eroded by the seemingly more urgent claims of other international communications media.... The American Council on Education ... urges that public policy support of scholarly exchanges should be strengthened, despite the present tensions. Indeed, this Board believes that both the Government of the United States and the academic community should strengthen their joint commitments to international intellectual communication and collaboration through this critical and lasting means.

Unfortunately, a constituency for international education in the United States is almost nonexistent, but two positive steps can be noted. A study of institutional policies on foreign students is being conducted by the American Council (supported by the Andrew W. Mellon Foundation), which is to be available in December 1981. New efforts by the exchange community—led by the Institute of International Education (IIE), the Council on International Educational Exchange, NAFSA, and thirteen other exchange organizations—to create a collaborative advocacy are intended to help awaken higher education leaders to the need for a more assertive, more coordinated, more appropriate institutional policy regarding international education. The International Educational Exchange Liaison Group, which resulted from this initiative, has issued a major position statement titled "Enhancing American Influence Abroad: International Exchanges in the National Interest."[2]

Assuming we live in an interdependent world, with critical global issues that require new knowledge, new techniques, and new understanding for their solution; assuming there are vast portions of the globe with basic educational needs required to lift them out of hunger and poverty; assuming Americans need to be able to communicate and relate increasingly on an international basis—then, perhaps the time has come to establish some clear standards and responsibilities for U.S. participation in international education.

Basic principles for effective international education need not be complicated. My association, NAFSA, is concerned with the international education perspective and practices of those who admit foreign students, teach them English, counsel them, and enrich their American experience through community experience. We in the association are concerned about the professional development of the people who perform these vital functions in the interchange process. Our 4,000 members practice within institutions whose leaders frequently do not know their work exists and who do not recognize that, for example, a thousand foreign students cannot have even their immigration requirements handled by a staff of two persons. Further, our people often feel cut off from faculty members with the most important influence on foreign students. Where foreign student advisors are successful in their work, they are almost always in institutions that have carefully decided which foreign students should be admitted, how they should be funded, what roles the students are to play in the central academic purposes of the institution, and what the foreign students' community involvements beyond the campus should be. In short, sound institutional policies generally assure good practices in foreign student advising, in the teaching of English as a second language, and in other functions throughout the international education process.

Principles and Guidelines for Self-Study

In a recent set of principles and a program of self-study, NAFSA leaders have attempted to provide guidance to institutions for international education exchange. NAFSA believes that all foreign

2. Available from IEELG, 1860 Nineteenth St., N.W., Washington, D.C. 20009.

participants in educational exchanges between the United States and other countries should be able to achieve the educational and personal goals they envision for their sojourn in the United States. NAFSA holds that professional staff who come in contact with participants in interchanges should be guided by a firm belief in the worth, dignity, and potential of every human being, regardless of national or ethnic origin, cultural or linguistic background, sex, race, social status, political affiliation, or religious belief. NAFSA holds that participants in educational interchanges should be able to learn as effectively and freely as possible, recognizing that the learning achieved in one culture is to be applied in others. And, NAFSA believes that, to promote the larger goals of educational interchanges, there is an increasing need for people of all countries to learn about one another and understand the conditions for interdependence.

What are some of the elements necessary to a comprehensive institutional policy regarding foreign students? The following considerations seem pertinent:

- The directional flow of students and scholars—who should go abroad; who should be admitted to the United States;
- The nature and scope of interchanges—how many should be students and how many scholars; what should be the emphasis on area studies; what should be the disciplines emphasized;
- The administrative location of services for foreign students and scholars within the host institutions.

Concerning the foreign student populations, attention should be given to:

- The ratio between U.S. and foreign students—What is an appropriate cultural mix?
- Geographic origin—Should the concentration be on a small number of specific countries or on a broad, general mix?
- Socioeconomic background—What financial aid will be provided to assure that essential, urgent academic study and research can be carried out? Is ability to pay the chief criterion?
- Academic qualifications—Do the students have the correct, acceptable credentials?
- Legal—Does the institution understand its obligations to comply with federal law and regulations?

The unplanned growth of foreign student enrollments, the exceptional problems of U.S. higher education during this period, the nation's worrisome international needs, and the world's extraordinary problems—all can lead to excessive wringing of hands. On the other hand, many splendid institutional examples display purposeful, healthy, effective foreign student programs—from relatively young community institutions like Broward Community College through Iowa State and the University of Minnesota to Stanford and MIT. There are splendid credential evaluation services (NAFSA professionals provided free evaluations last year for thousands of applicants to institutions having fewer than fifty foreign students); the American Association of Collegiate Registrars and Admissions Officers and NAFSA have provided excellent manuals on the admission of foreign students. The National Liaison Committee of IIE, AACRAO, the College Board, the Council of Graduate Schools, and NAFSA have set up a national clearinghouse on recruiting activities. NAFSA maintains a Home Country Employment Registry now used by some four hundred corporations. The Council on International Educational Exchange is strengthening its already excellent study abroad programs, and Georgetown University has recently established a new International Student Exchange Program to stimulate undergradate study in countries not traditionally a part of U.S. study abroad. NAFSA and numerous professional societies have been collaborating on a series of symposia on the relevancy of U.S. higher education.

There are already in foreign student affairs some exceptional achievements such as the Fulbright program and some embarrassing practices such as those of certain headhunters abroad. However, most of the process is as yet neither very good, nor very bad.

The stakes in international education are now too high to allow the whole process to develop haphazardly without clear institutional objectives. Howard Enarson summed it up well in his IIE speech when he said, "For the most part we are without a plan, system, or strategy." While a coherent national policy for international education seems unlikely in the near future, it is clearly time for those communities in the academy and in official sectors to take some greater charge of this unparalleled educational opportunity.

American Council on Education

The American Council on Education, founded in 1918 and composed of institutions of higher education and national and regional education associations, is the nation's major nongovernmental coordinating body for postsecondary education. Through voluntary and cooperative action, the Council provides comprehensive leadership for improving educational standards, policies, procedures, and services.